OWN THE MICRO

OWN THE MICROPHONE

How 50 of the World's Best Professional Speakers Launched Their Careers (And How You Can, Too!)

Created and Compiled by

BRIDGETT McGOWEN

BMc TALKS

Dedication

To Aaron and Parker

Acknowledgment

Simone, you're always right ... about everything. You're the best.

Do You Want to Get Published?

"You should write a book."

Either you've heard it or you've said it, but at BMcTALKS Press, we believe you should do it.

We take your dream from a great idea to a beautifully formatted book.

BMcTALKS Press is an independent publishing company that's fully committed to getting your non-fiction work published in a timely manner and providing you with a finished product that's professionally done and one of which you will be proud.

When you submit your manuscript to BMcTALKS Press, you receive personal attention, a fair price, and one of the higher author royalties in the industry.

This will be one of the most exciting experiences ever.

You're an expert. Now it's time you let everyone know it.

Visit www.bmtpress.com to schedule a complimentary ideation call and to get you FREE author's guide.

Let's print your passion!

Public Speaker

A person who is regarded as an orator, rhetorician, eulogist, facilitator, lecturer, or speechmaker who regularly speaks in public; one who knows and practices the art of effective oral communication with large, small, face-to-face, and/or virtual audiences.

Professional Speaker

A person who is regarded as an orator, rhetorician, eulogist, facilitator, lecturer, or speechmaker who regularly speaks in public; one who knows and practices the art of effective oral communication with large, small, face-to-face, and/or virtual audiences …

and who gets paid for doing so.

Dear Go-Getter ...

Thank you for adding a copy of this book to your personal library. That means a lot to all the book's contributors.

We are extremely excited for you and what this step means for your personal growth and your professional future.

Congratulations on investing in yourself and valuing your development. You are SO worth it!

Now, get ready to own the microphone!

Share the Knowledge

Get this book for a go-getter FRIEND, COLLEAGUE, FAMILY MEMBER, or COLLEGE GRAD.

Own the Microphone: How 50 of the World's Best Professional Speakers Launched Their Careers (And How You Can, Too!) gives you a blueprint for exactly how to launch your professional speaking business—either as a full-time effort or as a part-time pursuit. Plus, you learn how 50 of the world's best professional speakers began their careers.

If you know of anyone who loves his/her profession and is truly talented, then it's time that person does more with that love and talent.

Whether it's an accountant, a coach, an entrepreneur, an educator, an engineer, a marketer, a sales expert, or a medical professional ... anyone in any industry who is passionate about it who is and highly knowledgeable in a field needs to have a professional speaking goal. This book details exactly how it's done, and get invaluable advice and guidance from the most amazing speakers on the planet.

And even if one has no interest in getting on a microphone or getting paid to speak, this one is a must-read. The stories of resiliency, pressing through when it feels like you cannot take another step, and embracing your unique power will move anyone.

Order your copies at **www.bmctalks.com/store** OR
www.bmtpress.com/press-room

Contact BMcTALKS Press at **info@bmtpress.com** for special bulk discounts for your audience!

Table of Contents

The Inspiration for *Own the Microphone*

In the course of one week in October 2019, I conducted multiple calls with speakers who were in the initial stages of launching their professional speaking careers, and they all wanted my answer to just one question: "How did you get started as a professional speaker?" This wasn't the first time I'd received this question or that I'd conducted such calls, and I enjoy them thoroughly. But here's wherein the disappointment came:

First, I was not walking away from these calls feeling 100% confident that I truly had been helpful, which got me to thinking.

What if my advice is not enough?

Oftentimes, I would find myself hanging up, energized by the thought I had offered good information but also realizing, a few minutes later, that I had inadvertently omitted a piece of advice that may have proven valuable. I would walk away from the calls, trying to figure out how to more consciously and concisely shape and organize the details surrounding my journey of being a professional speaker in a way that outlined a clear path for others when I had to answer the question again in the future..

Then it hit me.

The reason I was leaving the calls unsure of my effectiveness was because I was not answering the real question they had. They did not really want my answer to "How did you get started as a professional speaker?"

They wanted to the answer to "Can I do this?!"

They wanted to know whether they have what it takes to own the microphone and were searching for nuggets that may have been buried in my story—nuggets that specifically resonated with their personal journeys—that would point them in the direction of what it takes to launch a professional speaking career.

In retrospect, I'm relatively certain my messages fell short and did not confirm for them that they can indeed do it, that they do have it in them. Shortly thereafter, this book project came to be: one resource that gives aspiring speakers valuable advice from not just one professional speaker but *multiple* professional speakers who know what it takes to successfully launch and grow a professional speaking career.

Listen. If you want to speak in a way that moves others to action, then you know you are destined for more. You know you are on to something and that you can do this on a bigger scale. You know you can positively impact others. You know this can be the start of something great. You know.

To anyone who's had a call or a face-to-face meeting with me, searching for answers, all you need to know is this: Yes, you can do it!

First, read "Your Blueprint: 25 Steps to Launch or Expand You Professional Speaking Career" to get everything I said in our conversation and, more importantly, everything I *wish* I'd said. Then dive in to get advice and inspiration from other professional speakers who know what it takes to own the microphone.

You've got this!

Bridgett McGowen
Creator of *Own the Microphone* and Founder of BMcTALKS, LLC

Your Blueprint: 25 Steps to Launch or Expand Your Professional Speaking Career
By BRIDGETT McGOWEN

International Professional Speaker | Forbes Contributor | Author | Publisher

Start here to get your blueprint of 15 must-do's and 10 nice to-do's. This is everything I wish had been outlined for me when I decided to become a full-time professional speaker. The recommendation is that you complete all the must-do's as soon as practical, then, prioritize and complete the nice-to-do's.

After you read this blueprint, dive into exploring how dozens of successful speakers launched their careers, and find inspiration for how to launch your own professional speaking career or how to take the next big step in your current journey of owning the microphone.

At this point, here is a word of caution: Be selective about the advice on which you take action. You will hear (and read) advice from many in the industry—this book included—and it can be difficult to ascertain exactly what you should do. Do not feel like you have to do everything or implement every great idea you hear or read right now, which be tempting, especially when starting out or when rebranding yourself.

Start at a level that's comfortable for you, and no matter what, keep moving forward.

15 Must-Do's

1. Confirm that being a professional speaker is really what you want to do. Oftentimes, you see only the glamorous side of the life of a professional speaker—the travel, the stages, the lights, the videos, the throngs of people listening to the speaker's message or waiting in line for a book signing and the opportunity to have a rare one-on-one conversation with the speaker. However, it involves a lot of work and the not-so-sexy behind-the-scenes components that you seldom see. In addition to talent, energy, and knowledge, you must be organized, focused, patient at times, and always ready to roll up your sleeves. The best way to determine if this is what you really want to do is to identify your mission—your why for doing this work. Is it because you want to make a difference? Do you want to heal others with your story? Do you want to move others to action? Do you want to transform people into leaders? Do you want to help audiences see the possibilities when it feels like there are none? Be honest as you find out why you want to do this, and you have your motivation for being a professional speaker; you will know if this is really what you want to do.

2. Write your business plan. You are establishing a business, so you need a plan for how it will look and operate and how you will consistently display your business to the public. At a minimum, detail your executive summary; the products and/or services you offer; your vision and mission statements; your business structure; a SWOT (strengths, weaknesses, opportunities, and threats) analysis; market analysis; sales and marketing strategy; financial projections; and your expansion and sustainability strategy. This is a lot of work, but it is your blueprint for how you will operate your business. You will be glad you completed this early on because it provides you clarity around creating a viable business.

3. Identify your speaking model. How will you approach your speaking business, and how will you hold yourself out to prospects so they know how to do business with you? For example, will you be a freelance subcontractor, a corporate trainer, a keynote speaker, or a motivational speaker? Knowing which model aligns with your business goals, personality, and presentation style will be integral in helping you focus your prospecting efforts.

4. Establish your speaking business as an entity that's separate from your personal self. This is another piece of the puzzle for establishing yourself as someone who's serious about the business. This means you need to register a Doing Business As (DBA) or a Limited Liability Corporation (LLC). And while you're at it, get an employer identification number (EIN) and set-up a business bank account, too. The DBA or LLC along with the EIN and the bank account are vitally important to keep business affairs from intermingling with your personal affairs and when filing your income taxes.

5. Purchase your URL, launch your website, and get your official email address. Purchase your URL so you can launch your website. When you build the website, to get started, it does not have to be elaborate or complicated, but do remember this is a representation of you; so do put some thought into it.

Get your email address to go along with it. It's just part of having that professional, polished look where people are emailing you at your domain as opposed to Gmail or the like. (Don't get me wrong; there's nothing problematic with conducting business using a Gmail email account or the like. It's good to have the email address that matches your website, though, if you are indeed intent on moving in the direction of being a professional speaker.)

6. Identify your signature or core message. What area of expertise do you have and is that on which you will speak? Figure out on what you want to be seen as an authority, then commit to delivering presentations focused on that core message. Notice I wrote "commit to delivering," not "commit to creating." Be smart with your time, and do not start designing presentations for which no one has asked. Create titles and descriptions for addition to the "topics" section of your website. When someone wants that topic, that's when you design the talk.

If you speak on a topic that is unfamiliar to most, then ensure you make it familiar so you capture the imagination. Here's what I mean: To what is your topic analogous? Think of how you can draw a connection between it and a topic or concept in mainstream society that would resonate with the general public. By drawing an analogy, you give your audiences a sense of familiarity with it.

Decide on the topic for which people will identify you as the go-to for answers and expertise.

7. Identify your target audience(s). Will you speak to corporations or associations? Will you work with individuals who pay by credit card (think Tony Robbins types of audiences) or those who invoice you? You may work with both, but most professional speakers focus on only one of them. Decide who wants and needs to hear your message. Find out where those people spend their time online and in-person and engage with them while holding out yourself as a professional speaker. Get in front of those with whom you know your message will resonate and who are willing to pay for your expertise.

8. Settle on what you will charge, and create your rates sheet. Naturally, if you have extensive experience speaking wherein you were not paid to speak in the past and are a beginner only in the sense that you are just launching your business, then your fee's starting point will look different from someone who may be an expert but is just beginning to take to the stage. In either instance, though, you will not charge the same for your twenty-first talk that you charged for your first talk.

The most important factors to take into consideration when creating your rate sheet is time and distance. Consider for how long you will speak; for how long, if at all, you are expected to engage with participants before and/or after your presentation; and how much time is involved with your travel to and from the presentation. With all those factors in mind, know what you will charge for a one-hour, two-hour, three-hour engagement, or full-day engagement. Know whether you are open to presenting webinars and what your fee is for that type of engagement. (By the way, I do not recommend offering a webinar that is longer than 60 to 90 minutes in length.) Consider if you will have a flat rate that includes travel expenses or if you will have a speaker fee plus a fee for travel, per diem, and hotel accommodations. Conduct an online search for speaking fee calculators; there are a few out there that do a great job of helping you determine your fees.

Additionally, consider the audience and how much pre-work you will need to perform beforehand. You can speak before certain audiences without needing to conduct extensive research about their needs and challenges, but there will be others who need to hear your message but about which you need more foundational knowledge on their backgrounds before you can successfully deliver a message that resonates.

Finally, decide if you will entertain other forms of compensation and what are those other forms of payment. If a client does not/cannot offer money as a means of payment, then (and if this is an engagement you really want to confirm) be ready to engage in a conversation about other ways you can be compensated for your work and expertise. To determine this, ask yourself "What else is valuable to my business? What besides money do I need to reach goals and/or continue to develop?"

9. Decide how often (or if) you will waive your fee. A number of factors can shape your decision here, and for many, it can be a sheer matter of finances. You may decide you will have a certain number of events in a year for which you will waive your speaking fee. You may aim to get in as many speaking engagements as you can so you can have footage of yourself or so you can have the speaking experience. There may be unpaid speaking engagements that present a strong propensity to lead to other opportunities. You may weigh the benefit of getting in front of an audience because someone will be in attendance you want to meet. The engagement may take place in a city you have always wanted to visit or one where you know you can conduct other business while in town. It may be an event that will be nice to have on your résumé, or there could be a big name also on the agenda, putting you in a position to say you spoke on the same program as him/her.

However, do not hesitate to decide to place a threshold on when you must absolutely charge to speak. Do not feel like you must waive your fee until someone decides to pay you. If someone contacts you and wants you to speak at an event, after you get the particulars and clarify the contact's goals and objectives for the speaking engagement and that you can indeed deliver, then do not hesitate to say, "Great! My fee is X."

There are event contacts who indicate they do not provide monetary compensation for you to speak but that they want you, and they tout the exposure you will gain by being on the agenda. In this instance, you have to weigh if "exposure" is a currency you value and/or if it is one that you need at that time. (Recall my aforementioned points: There may be unpaid speaking engagements that present a strong propensity to lead to other opportunities. You may weigh the benefit of getting in front of an audience because someone will be in attendance you want to meet. The engagement may take place in a city you have always wanted to visit ....) At the same time, though, there are many professional speakers who are seasoned, who perform this work full-time, and who will tell you in a heartbeat that they cannot feed their families a bowl of exposure or pay a bill with it.

Talking price can make some uncomfortable; do know it gets easier with time, and understand this: you are getting paid not for the 60 or 90 minutes you are in front of that audience; you are getting paid for the hours, days, weeks, months, years, and decades of expertise, talent, skill, and genius you bring to the microphone. Own it.

10. Regularly reach out to meeting planners and organizations with your pitch. Commit to targeting the right meeting planners—those who plan and organize events for your target audience—and contact a set number each day. Have a clean, succinct pitch that focuses more on the benefits to the event planner and his/her audience than it focuses on you. Have a plan for this outreach, and be consistent with and diligent about your outreach as it is one of the most crucial strategies for landing speaking engagements.

11. Always have a contract in place. Business—especially of the four-, five-, and six-figure type—cannot be done with only a handshake and a smile. You need a reliable paper trail. Outline not only your fee, but also the deliverables, details of the engagement, and all terms and conditions. Leave nothing to chance. Make it very clear what you will do in exchange for the speaker fee, any policies about videotaping, whether you require a deposit and in what amount, cancellation clauses, and specific dates. So much can go into the contract. My attitude is we can talk all day about what an event contact wants, but the gig is not confirmed until the contract is signed and the deposit has cleared the bank.

12. Get photos and videos of yourself in action as much as possible. You will want to have these on your website because words (written testimonials) tell only so much of the story. People need to see and hear what it would be like to have you on their stages.

13. Get testimonials from satisfied audience members. It's one thing for you to say how dynamite you are, but it's an entirely different game when *others* talk about how you owned the room and made a difference. Again, written testimonials are good, but video testimonials are even better.

14. Get involved in your profession, grow professionally, and expand your network. One of the best investments you can make in yourself and in your business is to become a member of professional organizations and surround yourself with others in the speaking industry who align with and are supportive of your professional mission. For starters, consider the National Speakers Association (NSA) and Toastmasters while understanding what to expect from each one.

At Toastmasters meetings, you get the opportunity to practice your speaking in front of peers and receive feedback on what worked well and how to improve. Keep in mind, though, that you will receive feedback from community partners and peers who may not be experts in presentation skills and public speaking, who may not be speaking coaches, and/or who may not be in the professional speaking business. Nonetheless, it is a great avenue for practicing your presentation material and getting in front of an audience on a regular basis.

NSA, on the other hand, has a very specific professional speaker focus; it helps people understand how to get in front of decision-makers, and how to build their speaking businesses. It is designed to provide tools and resources to support professional speakers with building thriving businesses. And the friends you make along the way in either organization will be absolutely priceless.

15. Take every speaking engagement seriously. Ensure you give a performance that sizzles. No matter if you are paid or not and regardless of the audience or the venue—it can be a retirement home—ensure you crush it so you do indeed have satisfied audience members. Additionally, by taking every speaking engagement seriously, you hone your skill, improve your delivery style, and you make it easier for event planners to refer you and your services to others.

10 Nice To-Do's

1. Create your brand or logo. Decide on, at a minimum, colors and fonts that will represent you and your brand so you have a consistent look for yourself and your speaking business. (Think about it; any well-known, national, or international brand uses the same colors and fonts so it is easily recognized. You want the same for yourself.)

You do not have to go so far as to have a logo, but it's nice to have for the aforementioned reasons. Enlist the help of a graphic designer, then use your brand/logo/colors/fonts on everything associated with your professional speaking business.

2. Have a professional photo shoot. If you are serious about being a real contender in the business, then schedule a professional photo shoot with a variety of poses for use on your website and in other marketing materials. Consider engaging the services of a professional wardrobe stylist, makeup artist, and hair stylist to have a quality product.

3. Get a professionally done speaker reel. This is also called a sizzle reel for the very reason that you want people to see you sizzling when you present! It is ideal if you locate a videographer who has worked with professional speakers before, so he/she will have a good idea of exactly what you want. Additionally, it is ideal to have the photo shoot and video shoot as one project with the same team of professionals previously listed.

4. Get professionally designed marketing materials. If you see yourself exhibiting at events where your target audience spends time, then you will want to invest in signage, table runners, banners, and the like to call attention to you and what you do. Additionally, a media kit (or press kit) proves beneficial as it serves as one document that encompasses the content on your website. If you have a prospective client that wants to recommend you as a potential speaker, then this document serves as a representation of what one would find on your website without one having to peruse your website. The professional photo shoot will come in handy in all instances mentioned herein.

5. Upgrade your business cards. Get business cards that are representative of your brand and the impression you want to give others when you hand over your card. The standard cards you can get at the local print shop are sufficient for getting started, but a higher-quality business card will catch people's attention and in a good way!

There are some who believe business cards are passé and not the most modern means of marketing a business. However, it never fails that the second I present my business card to someone who requests it and when it lands in the person's hand, I get a reaction. Either the high-quality feel of the card itself and/or the energetic picture of me on the reverse side elicits a positive response. Every time. Every single time. So here's my take: Business cards may not be the sexiest or most revolutionary twenty-first century marketing tool, however, what will never go out of style is any additional opportunity to make a positive impression with yourself and your brand.

6. Hire an assistant. My preference is a virtual assistant (VA) because she/he works from the comfort of home or another location of personal choice and does not need you to supply an office or equipment. A VA can perform a number of tasks for you that free you up to do what you love to do, which is design and facilitate amazing presentations. One of the most important tasks you can have your VA perform is prospecting for you. While you are on a stage, he/she can be behind the scenes, contacting event managers and the like, setting up calls, and booking your next engagement.

7. Have reliable legal representation in your list of contacts. You may never need him/her, but it is smart to have a firm that will represent you and look out for your business interests. Besides, having an attorney on hand to review contracts, for example, can be priceless, and the fee you pay the attorney is a fraction of the contract value. (I know this firsthand from a time I had a client that did not want to use my contract but had a standard contract it used with speakers. I immediately enlisted the help of an attorney to conduct the contract review and to ensure it was fair for both parties and that it included my requirements.)

8. Make it easy for prospective clients to get in touch with you. This is nice to have so you are not going back and forth with prospective clients via email, trying to locate a good time on both of your calendars to speak. When you have an online scheduler account, you can send prospects a link that takes them directly to your calendar and your availability so they can choose what works for both your calendar and their calendars.

9. Make it easy for your followers to stay in touch with you. Social media is nice, but if you blog or if you plan to host events yourself, for example, then your fans will want to hear and read your advice and expertise and/or know what you're doing. Invite audience members to sign-up to be on your email list, then stay in touch with them.

10. Create multiple revenue streams. If you crush it with your presentations, then people simply want more of you and more of your insight. Having additional offerings that connect to your presentation topic is an excellent avenue for giving your audience more. Not only do additional offerings provide you with other revenue streams, but they also put you in a position to again be seen as an authority, and they put you in a position to deliver even more value to your audiences.

Have questions?
What to discuss these steps in further detail?

Visit **www.callwithbridgett.com** to book a no-obligation call with Bridgett McGowen to receive personal and helpful guidance.

It'll be the best 30 minutes you ever spent working on your speaking business.

No one in this world does what you do
the way you do it.

No one.

Own your story.
Own your success.
Own your genius.
Work your given magic.

Own the microphone.

SECTION 1

1
The Very Dark Parts of My Past Are the Very Parts That Made Me Extraordinary
By STACY BERNAL
Speaker | Author | Coach | Disruptor at See Stacy Speak, LLC

How I Got My Start

I often begin presentations by telling my audience I'm an "award-winning" speaker. Then I click to a slide that shows a picture of a newspaper clipping of 14-year-old me, grinning widely, eyes half-closed, sitting with a group of other kids and a few teachers from Sedgefield Middle School with a medal around my neck. The audience always gets a chuckle out of this little bit. I joke that eighth grade had been a good year for me, explaining that, in addition to winning my first public speaking competition, later that year I would go on to become the first chair clarinetist for the South Carolina All-State Band. Basically, I say, I pretty much peaked that year.

And there is some truth to that statement, but there is also a darker underlying current to that same story. Because while I had some great accomplishments in 1991, it had also been one of the worst, most tumultuous years of my life, too. What I didn't know then was how the shifting tides of those hard days would come back and resurface in surprising ways later in my life.

In 1991, my parents divorced—not your standard, run-of-the-mill divorce either. My father's transgressions spanned over more than a decade and left many victims in his wake; I was just one of the many. My parents sold the home they had built together, and my mom moved my three siblings and me into a single-wide mobile home. What my family went through at the time was difficult and heartbreaking. But it would be another 30 years before I would recognize that period as "traumatic." In the meantime, I knew that my family now had secrets, and I knew that these were things we didn't talk about. So, I went about my life, silently shouldering the burden of shame, masking the darkness with jokes and comedic relief. No one had any idea the pain I had buried beneath my witty and sarcastic personality.

I was the drum major of my high school marching band my junior year when I found out I was pregnant. I grew up Mormon in a small, southern town, so my pregnancy predicament was juicy gossip. I had decided to place my baby for adoption, which, like my ever-growing belly, I tried to keep secret. One day I walked into a bathroom stall and saw that someone had scribbled in black Sharpie that I was a "knocked up hoe." I felt ashamed, embarrassed, and hurt. In that moment, I decided I would graduate early so I wouldn't have to go back for my senior year.

In order to do that, I had to sign up for summer school classes. There was a strict attendance policy that in order to graduate, a student couldn't miss more than two days. I went into labor on a Wednesday evening, gave birth to a beautiful boy on Thursday, placed him with his parents on Friday, and was back in school the next Monday. A few weeks later I graduated high school and got my first job working at a movie theater. I started partying with all my co-workers, numbing the pain of my past by finding a short-lived euphoria at the bottom of bottles of Zima. This was the start of years of a downward spiral so that, by my thirty-first birthday, I was a three-time college dropout going through my third divorce. I had lost custody of my then 12-year-old daughter, and my three-year-old son had just been diagnosed with autism.

By the fall of 2009, I was at rock bottom—hopeless, on government assistance, living paycheck to paycheck. I couldn't see the light at the end of the tunnel. Except that, in May of that same year, I had run my first marathon. That experience had sparked a tiny bit of hope for my life; if I could run 26.2 miles, I was capable of hard things. I could figure out a way to get myself out of the gutter. With practically no money to my name, I filed my Free Application for Federal Student Aid (FAFSA) application and applied to the local college, Weber State University. In January of 2010, I started my fourth (and final) attempt at college. In 2013, I graduated summa cum laude and was named the Outstanding Graduate for my major.

Despite my slowly growing list of achievements, I still could never quite shake the feelings of inadequacy I always felt about myself. I knew I was the trailer park trash, abused, "knocked-up hoe." My limiting beliefs told me that if people really knew about my past and who I was, then no one would like me. I could never fully stand in my story because I was ashamed of so many parts of it. Shame shackled me into silence. Then, in 2017, an opportunity arose for me to share some of my story at a luncheon for business associates. This was my chance: a place I could test the waters of owning my past. I called my presentation "Failure to Finisher" and practiced for hours, sharing how running my first marathon changed the trajectory of my life.

On the day of the luncheon, I fully expected that I would face some backlash. Never before had I stood in front of an audience and talked about my unplanned teen pregnancy and subsequent adoption. And these were people I knew professionally. What I did *not* expect was the outpouring of love, support, kindness, and connection I received. People came up to me after the presentation and shared their own stories of mishaps and mistakes. One friend told me I should write a book. I laughed at him that day. But in September of 2019, I'm proud to say I published my first book, *The*

Things We Don't Talk About: A Memoir of Hardships, Healing and Hope.

From that first presentation, my speaking career was born. I got invited to speak for teen girls, school districts, women's groups, corporate retreats, recovering drug addicts, and at-risk youth. I found purpose in sharing my story as a means to help others in their own journeys. The very dark parts of my past that I felt had diminished me were, in fact, the very parts that made me extraordinary. It lights my soul on fire to help others feel that same way about themselves. The girl whose goofy grin graced *Goose Creek Gazette* in eighth grade isn't back—she was there all along.

My Advice to Aspiring Professional Speakers

The one piece of advice I would give to new speakers is to know your message, know your WHY, and know your audience. So many other facets of your business will ebb and flow but staying true to these tenets will help you connect to those whose lives you're meant to touch. There will be hard days that make you question what you're doing. Wake up every day with your WHY at the top of mind. Trust the process.

ABOUT STACY

Stacy Bernal is a speaker, author, and personal development coach at See Stacy Speak, LLC. She graduated summa cum laude from Weber State University (WSU) with a B.A. in Public Relations and Advertising and was named the 2013 Outstanding Graduate for her major. She proudly serves on the WSU Alumni Association Board of Directors and the Ogden/Weber Chamber's Women in Business Executive Board.

Stacy has been featured on Thrive Global, ChicagoNow, Scary Mommy, *Autism Parenting Magazine*, and *HER Magazine*. She recently published her first book, *The Things We Don't Talk About: A Memoir of Hardships, Healing, and Hope.* From once-a-bartender to now-a-board-member, she feels purposeful about sharing her message of triumph, inspiration, and empowerment. She is the creator of Awesome Autistic Ogden, an autism appreciation event turned community resource, as well as a 501(c)(3) nonprofit, Bernal Badassery Foundation.

Stacy lives happily with her family and fur babies near the mountains where she enjoys all the amazing outdoor recreation Ogden, Utah has to offer like running marathons, triathlons, relay races, and an ultra-marathon. She loves to travel and looks forward to many great adventures all over the world.

LESSONS LEARNED FROM STACY

What caught your attention? What are your takeaways?

2
The Difference Between a Good Speaker and a GREAT Speaker
By BRIAN BIRO
America's Breakthrough Coach | Professional Speaker | Best-Selling Author

How I Got My Start

I did not become a professional speaker out of the desire to be up in front of big audiences espousing great wisdom. In fact, when I began presenting, I had very little idea of what a motivational speaker was. And yet, as I look back, I had been carefully preparing for this career I love so dearly throughout my entire adult life. Becoming a professional speaker was simply the culmination of discovering who I truly am!

I attended Stanford University long ago (we won't mention any years!) and like most young people going to college I was trying to figure out what I was going to do with this thing called my life. And though I loved Stanford and the challenge of such an extraordinary environment, I quickly discovered that what I loved most was not at college. What I loved most was what I did in the summers to help put myself through Stanford (that and mega-loans, which I didn't love!) The pursuit that consumed me so fully each summer was teaching and coaching swimming. I absolutely loved it! I'd start the summer with a group of little kids who had no idea what they were doing. They had learned very little stroke-technique, they'd never been a part of real team, and never set goals to pursue. I was eighteen, nineteen, years-old and so full of enthusiasm that you'd accurately describe me as an "Ooh, ooh, ooh guy!"—you know, that fellow you grew up with who, when asked a question simply couldn't control his enthusiasm and would bubble out, "Ooh, ooh,

ooh, call on ME!" I poured my full heart and soul into coaching these kids and by the end of each summer they would improve so much, both individually and collectively, that I couldn't put them out of my mind when I headed back to school.

So, when the time came to graduate, my buddies thought I was crazy because they were going to medical school, law school, or business school, and though I had been fortunate enough to do well at Stanford, I made up my mind that I was going to live my life doing that which I loved. And it was clear that what I loved was coaching. So that's exactly what I did.

I started my own swimming team in Southern California. It was a U.S. swim team which meant unlike at a school where I'd work with the kids for a season or semester, I was a part of these young peoples' lives year-round. When I started, we had about fifteen little kids, almost all between the ages of seven and nine-years-old. But for the next eight years, that team was my life. And let me make a promise to you about the power of your focus. If you put your full heart and soul into ANYTHING with what's really inside of you for *eight years*, incredible things can happen.

Over the course of those eight years we grew from a tiny novice team to one of the largest privately-owned swimming teams in the country, numbering nearly 275 swimmers. We earned national recognition by placing in the top 10 at the Senior Nationals, and the top three twice in a row at the Junior National Championships. I received the US Swimming Coaching Excellence Award, and more than forty of our athletes earned college scholarships to schools across the country from the University of Hawaii to the University of Miami. Some of our top performers participated in the Olympic Trials and international competitions.

What I didn't realize at the time was that the heart of my role as head coach was motivational speaking. Every single day I delivered extemporaneous, heartfelt, passionate, inspirational messages to these young people about their potential. Somehow, I understood that I wasn't really coaching swimming, I was coaching PEOPLE. The most important journey in life is only about eighteen inches … the distance from the head to the heart. Great speaking is about helping others arrive at that destination.

My Advice to Aspiring Professional Speakers

To me, the difference between a good speaker and a GREAT speaker comes down to two vital keys: Authenticity and Passion! Authenticity as a speaker is only possible when you release the need for approval. This may sound completely looney to most aspiring speakers because at the heart of the most prevalent desire to enter this career is the vision of receiving standing ovations and being adored by audiences. But, like politicians who discard their principles for big financial contributions and influential backers in order to get elected, speakers who are driven by the need for approval pay a massive price … their true authenticity.

Now please do not misunderstand me. I love the appreciation I receive from participants at my presentations. I am truly grateful for their kind words and passionate positive feedback. But it is not why I speak. It is not at the heart of my motivation. The reason I love speaking so dearly is 100% because of the way I feel when I am presenting. I feel that I am doing what I have been put on earth to do. I feel the pure joy of servant leadership where my inspiration is to give, not to get. Mother Teresa said, "Service is love in action." When I am speaking, I am fully present, offering my full heart and the best I have to give without trying to force or manipulate a response. I often joke (though it's actually totally true) that when I'm on stage I'm twenty-five again. As soon as I finish, I'm back to sixty-five!

True passion can only come when you are fully authentic. So, these two secrets of great speaking are intertwined. You must love your stories and relish the truth that when you tell them well, your stories become their story. They see their children, their challenges, and their triumphs through yours. When people come up to you and thank you for changing their lives, deeply appreciate their spirit and kindness, but recognize that your role is as a catalyst not a transformer. The truth is that they have felt your passion and resonated with your message and now are ready to change their own lives! Offer your stories and ideas as if they were dishes at a grand brunch buffet. It is up to the participants to choose which they will devour and convert to new energy!

ABOUT BRIAN

Brian Biro is America's Breakthrough Coach! He is one of the nation's foremost speakers and teachers of Leadership, Possibility Thinking, Thriving on Change, and Team-Building. He has delivered more than 1,800 presentations around the world in the past twenty-nine years. His clients include such diverse organizations as Lockheed Martin (94 events!), the US Army, the University of Notre Dame, UCLA, the North Carolina Association for the Association for the Advancement of Teaching, senators and representatives from thirteen western states, the Virginia School Superintendents, Kaiser Permanente, Starbucks, Pizza Hut, IHOP, Microsoft, Oracle, Cisco, McDonalds, Dairy Queen, Allstate

Insurance, Good Samaritan Hospital, RE/MAX, Shaklee, the American Rental Association, and hundreds more. A major client offered the best introduction about Brian's impact when he said, "Brian Biro has the energy of a ten-year-old, the enthusiasm of a twenty-year-old, and the wisdom of a seventy-five-year-old." A former vice-president of a major transportation corporation in the Pacific Northwest, he helped lead a major turnaround that resulted in the company quadrupling in revenues, becoming solidly profitable, and being named the leader in the air freight industry for customer service and convenience by *Distribution Magazine*. In his first career, Brian built one of the largest private swim teams in the U.S., numbering over 275 competitive swimmers. His team finished in the top three on three occasions at the Junior National Championships, the top 10 at the Senior National Championships, and forty-four of his athletes earned full college scholarships. He received the United States Swimming National Coaching Excellence award given to the top 10 American Swimming coaches.

Brian is the author of 14 books including best-seller, *Beyond Success!* which reached #16 on the Amazon.com top 100—from over 2 million titles, and his new book, *There Are No Overachievers.* Brian was rated #1 from over 40 speakers at four consecutive INC. Magazine International Business Conferences. He graduated with honors from Stanford and served as the President of the UCLA Graduate School of Management Student Association while earning his MBA from UCLA. He has appeared on Good Morning America, CNN's Business Unusual, and has been a guest on more than 300 radio programs throughout the country. He has been a featured speaker at the Disney Institute in Orlando. Brian was named one of the UCLA Graduate School of Management's 100 Most Inspirational Graduates in the history of the school. Most recently Brian was also honored as one of the top 65 Motivational Speakers in the world.

LESSONS LEARNED FROM BRIAN

What caught your attention? What are your takeaways?

3
Just Take Action: Do Not Allow Fear to Stop You
By BRIAN BOGERT
President/Owner of The Brian Bogert Companies, LLC

How I Got My Start

I have told the story so many times that startled looks and speechless reactions don't phase me one bit. As a child, I quickly realized that anyone who asked "*What happened to your arm?*" expected to hear about a playground accident or sports injury—not the raw truth: "*I got run over by a truck, and my arm was torn off.*" Needless to say, I never let what could have been a lifelong handicap slow me down. I learned a long time ago to not get stuck by what has happened to me but get moved by what I can do with it.

I was seven years old without a shy bone in my body and a story that was extremely unique. For that reason, I was put on stages from that time forward to provide perspective, motivation, and direction to all of those around me. The speaking itch hit me early on when I realized the power of a great story and how it could shape people's thoughts, feelings, and lives. So, I continued on the speaking path (unpaid) for the next twenty years.

After a successful decade in the insurance business, my wife and I had our first kid. I have always had a crazy work ethic and relentless drive to be able to provide for my family. The problem I now faced is that providing for a family without any physical presence isn't really providing. I was burning the candle at both ends and had not adjusted my life appropriately when my son entered the world. So, I realized I had a problem and needed help to fix it. I hired my first coach.

A month into working with him, he said, "Brian, you need to be speaking and coaching professionally." I honestly blew off the comment because at the time, I was so focused on figuring out how to be present as a father while also continuing to grow my business, the last thing I wanted was to add something else to my plate. Over the course of the following nine months, he continued to trickle the message and nudge me down the speaking and coaching path. Turns out, he was right, and I am forever grateful.

In 2015, I officially launched my speaking and coaching business and have been humbled by the response and support. I had a phenomenal mentor in my coach who challenged me and helped shift portions of my story to make the messages even stronger. Since then, I have become a student of my craft and have found that being on stage and having the ability to truly impact people's lives is one of my happy places. Although I have been speaking for nearly thirty years, and have been a professional speaker for five, this journey is just beginning for me.

My Advice for Aspiring Professional Speakers

The biggest piece of advice for aspiring professional speakers is to just take action to get on stage. Many people are drawn to speaking, have a unique story, and are passionate about and/or are an expert on a topic but never put themselves in a position to speak. There are many reasons people do not get started; they may be afraid of public speaking, they may feel no one wants to listen to them, they may not know how to get on stages, they may feel their speech isn't perfect, and the list goes on... Just get started. If any of the above reasons sound like you, here are a couple tips.

First and foremost, do not wait for anything to be perfect. Perfection is the enemy of progress. This does not mean I am suggesting you don't need to be prepared and practiced, but I find that we often learn more from mistakes than successes. So, if you wait until you think things are perfect, you will never get started because perfection doesn't exist, and think about all the lessons you would miss along the way.

Second, do not allow fear to stop you. Most of the greatest things in life are just on the other side of fear. I get it; standing in front of a group of people can be nerve racking. Every single time I take the stage, I feel nervous. Those nerves used to stay with me almost the entire time I was on stage, but now they are pretty much gone by the end of the first couple sentences. The fear in our heads is always worse than what we actually experience.

Third, not knowing how to do something isn't a reason to not learn how. Being vulnerable and asking for help is stronger than doing nothing. There are many resources available to people desiring to be professional speakers. If you need help structuring your talk, getting comfortable in front of groups, getting feedback on your content, learning how to get on stages, etcetera, there are organizations and people to help. There are organizations like Toastmasters and National Speakers Association that help people with all of the above and more. One of the other greatest resources to new and existing speakers? Other speakers! Find a mentor or a coach. Ask for advice, then implement. Those who are the best at anything in life get help and get coached.

So, remember:
1. Take action. If you feel the desire to speak, start speaking.
2. Don't wait for perfection. Focus on making progress towards your goal.

3. Everyone feels fear and nerves. It is the worst for the first few sentences, then it dwindles.
4. Get coached. Find resources and learn from others.

Best of luck to you! I'll look forward to seeing you on stage someday!

ABOUT BRIAN

Brian's miraculous healing from a fully detached (and re- attached) arm taught him early in life that awareness, intentionality, and authenticity are the ointment that binds to success and human connection.

Today, Brian is a professional speaker and human behavior and performance coach to executives, entrepreneurs, athletes, and others looking to unlock what is inside. He lives his life by the "if and how I can help" principle, which impacts everything he touches. His ability to provide energy and encouragement to those he interacts with inspires them to make their best even better. The foundation for his work is to help others become more aware and more intentional so they can become who they already are, their most authentic selves. These are essential for becoming a positive leader across business, community, and family.

In addition to speaking and coaching, Brian helps lead and expand the Phoenix office of Lockton Companies—a global insurance brokerage firm. Brian's deep expertise and community-minded focus make him a strategic advocate for helping people protect and build their businesses. Prior to joining Lockton, he was responsible for mentoring new producers across the nation at a publicly traded brokerage firm.

He has been recognized as one of "40 Under 40" by the *Phoenix Business Journal* and regularly as a top performer in the Southwest. He is a founding member of the Vinnies—a professional advisory board that he helped populate with motivated members who are advancing the philanthropic capacity of St. Vincent de Paul. He also serves on the boards or advisory committees of American Cancer Society, Adelante Healthcare, TGEN, United Blood Services, the YMCA, Scottsdale Leadership, Valley Leadership and is founder of the Phoenix Children's Hospital Patient & Family Alumni Leadership (PALs) group—the very hospital that so carefully aided his healing with an expectation of excellence. In 2013, Brian co-created a mobile app to help children understand confusing medical terms involved in their care. With more than 12,000 downloads in over 100 countries, Brian's work delivered upon the "if and how I can help" principle with a lasting legacy for the patients behind him.

Brian is a Phoenix native and proud father of two young children with his beautiful wife. Brian will tell you that being a dad is the most meaningful thing he has ever done, and he understands well the importance of work-life integration that so many clients seek. He believes with awareness, focus, and intentionality you can have it all!

LESSONS LEARNED FROM BRIAN

What caught your attention? What are your takeaways?

4
LOVE Your Subject
By DEBBIE BOONE
President, 2 Manage Vets, LLC

How I Got My Start
It is my belief that all humans are professional speakers. If you have a job that faces the public, it is very handy to know how to present your "pitch" with confidence and authority.

I grew up serving the public in my family's restaurant. From childhood, I was immersed in attending to people, and I learned early in life how to make people happy. However, being in the restaurant business was far removed from my goal of being a veterinarian. I focused my studies in the sciences, and when I was accepted into the PreVet curriculum at North Carolina State University, I was thrilled. My plan to be in NCSU's first veterinary school class was delayed by some local politics that slowed the building of the school. When I graduated, I returned to the restaurants and married my high school sweetheart.

Caring for animals was still my calling, so when we moved to another town for my husband's job, I ran around to all the vet clinics and applied for jobs. Thanks to the outstanding barbequed ribs we sold, the manager of one of the practices routinely came to eat at our restaurant. She remembered my service and took a chance on me with a part-time receptionist position. I was in heaven! I worked at minimum wage for about six months until my bank account told me I had better find higher paying work.

I moved to retail management—first, a fabric shop, then a jewelry department in a big box store. One day, I sold a watch to one of the associate vets at the practice where I had worked. Two days later, I received a call from my former boss explaining to me that his wife was insisting he hire a practice manager because she was sick of him coming home at 10:00pm or 11:00pm every night. I interviewed, got the job, and ran the practice for nineteen years.

During those years, I brought my knowledge of customer service and hospitality into the staff training. This was unusual for a medical facility and still is from my personal experience in human medical offices.

This connection and relationship building with our clients resulted in a preventive care compliance rate almost 40% above industry norms. Pharmaceutical sales reps were very interested in how we had managed this amazing statistic. They came to me wanting to know if I thought I could teach others this magic formula. I had always led our team meetings and training, so I said, "Yes." I was definitely pushing myself out of my comfort zone.

It began with small projects like roundtable discussions then advanced to facilitation of the tables. I was asked to develop a presentation on change implementation and how we had managed to move our doctors, staff, and clients from an older product to a newer and better solution. Once the program was created, the pharmaceutical company had me come in to train two other veterinary managers. They also gave us professional media training by a local news anchor. I firmly believe there is nothing more uncomfortable than seeing and hearing yourself on camera. I did win the day by almost never saying, "um," "like," or "you know!" Once my training was done, I was asked to give a one-hour presentation to a group of veterinarians—in Puerto Rico. Yes, my first big public speech was to over 400 veterinarians in a tropical paradise. Then, believe it or not, I got to go back three weeks later and do it again.

After that, I changed jobs and took the COO position for a very large mixed animal practice. I was speaking at random small events. I would take my dog and go to the local schools and speak on good pet care. I was interviewed on the local radio about pets and on TV about the shelter animals, as our practice also managed the county facility.

Shortly after I started my new job, I got a call from one of the managers who had taken the media training with me. She was working as a consultant in a practice and wanted me to come help with the "people" part as it had always been my focus and strength. I declined because I couldn't break away, but we kept in touch.

Then 2008 hit. I was laid off. Even though I had developed a large network of veterinary connections who knew and admired my skills, I couldn't find a job. No one was hiring. Of course, I had severance and unemployment and now a prime opportunity to do what I always wanted—to start a consulting business focusing on customer service and communication skills. Randomly, I reached back out to my consultant friend who had asked me for help. She was working on a project that she couldn't reveal but instructed me to "not take a job—I have something for you." She was right.

Two months later, she called me to let me know she had created a receptionist training program that the second largest veterinary distribution company in the US was going to launch, and she wanted me to teach it. I jumped at the chance.

The rest is history. I began teaching the class in 2009 and have now taught more than 10,000 veterinary staff members and have presented in almost every state. In addition, I have created multiple presentations for pharmaceutical companies, national conferences, and private hospitals. I have become extremely comfortable in front of an audience, and I believe that it shows in the responses I get after the sessions.

My Advice to Aspiring Professional Speakers

If I were to give an aspiring speaker any advice it would have to be— LOVE your subject. Because I have generalized management knowledge, I can present on multiple topics, but the best presentations are the ones that light a fire in my heart. People don't want talking heads; they want someone with whom they can relate and connect. They want to know you understand their problems and are bringing knowledge to the table that improves their lives.

You won't connect with everyone. That is all right. Some people come to a presentation with a willing mind and others are there under duress. If the material is good, you can often catch the attention of the forced attendees but not always. Take the feedback as something to use to learn and improve. I confess sometimes it hurts to pour so much energy and effort into a presentation to have someone say you were "okay" or worse. If you can look at the information with a clinical eye and not your emotional heart, you will probably learn something you can use to make your material better. To give you an example, I was raised in a very high-end veterinary practice and learned to promote the absolute best care for my patients. We were also considered expensive. This made me a self-professed "medical snob." But my audience typically does not work in that type of practice. It is possible they work in high-volume, lower cost, minimal care clinics. I learned from feedback surveys that my occasional remarks about lower quality care was alienating some of my audience members. Keep in mind I am teaching communication skills, not medicine. I adjusted and softened my approach by confessing my bias, acknowledging that there is a place for everyone, and creating additional scenarios focused on low-cost care.

Learning to be a profession speaker is always a work in progress. I never think I am finished learning how to be better. My advice is read and study the skills of presenting, then practice. I record my presentations on my laptop and play them back so I can embed the material in my brain by reading and listening. Know your subject so that when someone asks you an off-topic question you can embrace it rather than fear it. Make connections with people who need your services by being brave enough to walk up to a stranger and introduce yourself. Tell stories from your experiences that people will relate to—this will make your material stick. Remember your audience wants you to succeed. They are rooting for you to be good. Talk with them like it is a conversation and they will connect and learn.

ABOUT DEBBIE

Debbie Boone, self-professed "customer service geek and champion for animal health," began her training in business management and customer care at 12 years old while working in her family's restaurants. A love of animals led her to a bachelor's degree in animal science from North Carolina State University and her first job in the industry as a client care representative at an animal hospital. Her business, retail, and hospitality background quickly moved her into hospital administration, and she managed American Animal Hospital Association (AAHA) accredited hospitals for 23 years. Her unique skillset includes experience working with a variety of veterinary hospitals, including small animal, mixed animal, specialty, and emergency practices. She also has experience with shelter management.

Debbie is considered an expert in team communication, the creation of positive practice culture, and the development of monthly paid wellness plans for veterinary practices. Acknowledged as a leader in change implementation and employee engagement, she has been sought out by major animal health manufacturers for her skills as a trainer and speaker.

During her presentations, Debbie incorporates real-life stories that resonate with attendees and lead to glowing reviews. Her impressive list of speaking engagements includes American Veterinary Medical Association (AVMA), WVC (formerly known as Western Veterinary Conference), AAHA, Midwest and Atlantic Coast Veterinary Conferences, and more. She has presented multiple VetFolio webinars and is the instructor for Patterson Veterinary Supply's Communication and Service class. Her frequent one-on-one contact with veterinary professionals keeps her abreast of the daily challenges veterinary practices face and the creative solutions they have found to overcome those challenges.

Debbie co-authored *The Veterinarian's Guide to Healthy Pet Plans— How to Design and Implement Successful Preventive Care Plans* and has been published in the Veterinary Hospital Managers Association (VHMA) newsletter, *Firstline*, *DVM 360* online, *Veterinary Team Brief*, *Trends Magazine*, and more. She is a member of VHMA, AAHA, VetPartners, and multiple veterinary business and management groups and also served on the AAHA LINC committee, assigned with selecting the AAHA Board of Directors. She is a member of the Board of Directors for VetPartners and the Fear Free[SM] Advisory Board and Speakers Bureau. Her latest project is the development of a Veterinary Practice Management concentration through the College of Agriculture and Life Sciences at North Carolina State University.

Debbie's business, 2 Manage Vets Consulting, helps practices develop extraordinary team communication and business skills to enhance patient care, improve profitability, and increase practice value. She strives to improve the lives of animals by using her expertise to improve workplace culture and the well-being of veterinary professionals.

In her spare time, Debbie enjoys reading, attempting to play golf, visiting the beach with her husband, traveling, and watching Atlantic Coast Conference (ACC) basketball.

LESSONS LEARNED FROM DEBBIE
What caught your attention? What are your takeaways?

5
You Are an Expert
By KATRINA BRITTINGHAM, JCDC, JCTC
Chief Executive Coach

How I Got My Start

I got started in the speaking business almost twenty years ago as a young minister in my local church. This gave me the confidence to speak at my corporate job, doing presentations and trainings for my team as well as a business owner later in my life, speaking on national and international events. Since my humble beginnings, I have spoken at various events and on diverse platforms both in-person and online.

My Advice to Aspiring Professional Speakers

My advice to anyone who is just starting out in the speaking arena is that you can do it. I am an introvert, and the misconception is that introverts don't make good speakers. Well, we do! Remember you are an expert, and people need and value what you bring to the table. Above all, have fun! Don't take yourself too seriously, meaning if you make a mistake, keep moving and laugh. It is okay to make the audience laugh, too. Even the most seasoned professionals get tongue-tied or make a mistake on stage from time to time. It is how you handle these moments that matter. People know you are human so they will be understanding. If you handle it with poise and a little humor, most will not remember the slip-up.

ABOUT KATRINA

Katrina Brittingham is an Executive and Career Transition Coach, author, public speaker as well as a radio and TV personality. She serves as Founder & CEO of VentureReady, LLC with a mandate of helping clients develop personally and professionally. Her career services firm provides clients with executive coaching, team engagement strategies, career coaching, and 360 assessments. She is also the owner of Venture Ready Broadcasting, an online radio and TV network.

She is the author of *Create an Interview Winning Résumé* and *The Complete Interview Readiness Guide: Build Confidence...Electrify the Room...Get Hired*! and is featured in "Modernize your Resume Get Noticed...Get Hired." Katrina frequently appears as a career expert on radio shows and has conducted workshops and training for the International Association of Women (IAW) and the National Society for Hispanic MBAs (NSHMBA). She is the host of CareerGPS - Global Positioning Strategies, an online radio show for senior leaders and executives who are looking to advance in their careers and High Tea With Me, an online tv show where leaders and entrepreneurs share provide expert advice.

In addition to the experience above, Katrina has almost two decades of experience in the field of health insurance, internal and external auditing, accounting, medical claims processing, process improvement, change management, and operations compliance.

Katrina earned both a Master of Business Administration and a Master of Accountancy degree from Rosemont College and the

University of Phoenix. She is also a Certified Professional Résumé Writer (CPRW) and a Job & Career Development Coach (JCDC), Job and Career Transition Coach (JCTC), as well as a certified Business Development and Marketing (BDM) coach.

LESSONS LEARNED FROM KATRINA
What caught your attention? What are your takeaways?

6
If It Is Your Passion, Then Do It
By LORI BRUHNS
Professional Productivity Speaker and Coach

How I Got My Start
After having my twins, I left my teaching career because the pay was less than childcare for two. I started my professional organizing company when they were one. About three years later, Duke University Health System called upon me to come speak about productivity, task management and organizational soft skills. I literally fell into it. In 2014, I transitioned from professional organizer to professional speaker.

My Advice to Aspiring Professional Speakers
I am working a full-time job and am a full-time speaker. If it is your passion, then do it … until you can do it as your primary income.

ABOUT LORI

Lori Bruhns is a multilingual accredited productivity coach and speaker. She is an expert in working with individuals who are ready to take control of their lives, get off the emotional rollercoaster, and finally accomplish their top priorities.

Through her personal coaching and keynotes, she has trained individuals at companies such as Duke University Health System, data analytics powerhouse SAS, and Rodan and Fields.

As a formally trained educator, Lori uses individualized strategies to help each unique client break down complex productivity problems into manageable bite size pieces.

Lori is available to work with clients who are stressed, tired, and overwhelmed to help them become more confident, empowered, and successful at home and work.

LESSONS LEARNED FROM LORI
What caught your attention? What are your takeaways?

7
Speaking is the Easy Part
By DAVID BRYSON
Speaker | Host of the Why Can't You? Podcast

How I Got My Start

I got started in the speaking business for two reasons in particular. First, I come from a background in theatre, improv, and sports broadcasting. This has been what I have trained to do professionally my whole life, and I thoroughly enjoy it. The author Malcolm Gladwell talks about putting in 10,000 hours to master a craft. I would not say I have speaking mastered, but I have put in the 10,000 hours.

Secondly, I bought a small business about four years ago. When I purchased the business, I felt there were a lot of things I didn't learn until after I signed on the dotted line. My goal in becoming a speaker was to pass on a lot of the lessons I have learned as an entrepreneur and help people avoid the same mistakes that I have made along the way.

My Advice to Aspiring Professional Speakers

Advice to other speakers is that for a long time, you will be the only one putting gas in your tank. If you're like me, then speaking is the easy part—5 % of the job. Lining up the gigs is the hard part—95% of the job. It's more emails and phone calls and follow-up than you ever imagined.

For people starting out, here is my number one piece of advice. Do not be afraid to speak for free at the beginning. No one is going to hire you until you have video of yourself. The best way to get video of yourself is to speak for free. Tell event planners you don't usually speak for free, but tell them you love their organization and would be happy to speak if you can bring a videographer. Do not tell event planners you speak for free, but you always want to make sure you set a value for your speaking services and that if you are not getting paid you are getting something else in return. Get your video edited; get a professional looking website; and then when you start emailing meeting planners, you are well on your way to booking gigs. I wish you success and do not give up! Why Can't You?

ABOUT DAVID

David Bryson is a keynote and motivational speaker who delivers an engaging and challenging message. He is called on to inspire, encourage, and help your organization get results.

David's speech can be tailored to meet the needs of your audience. Some favorite topics of his include, "storyselling," teamwork, and the importance of giving. David brings a diverse background from a career in corporate life to being an entrepreneur. His well-rounded background guarantees he connects with everyone in your audience.

David is the host of the top rated "Why Can't You?" podcast. "Why Can't You?" features guests from around the world who help to educate and inspire listeners by sharing their stories and, especially, the lessons they learned during their journey to get where they are today.

LESSONS LEARNED FROM DAVID

What caught your attention? What are your takeaways?

8
Speak for Impact, Not Applause
By ISHA COGBORN
Personal Brand Strategist | Author | Media Host | Speaker | Coach | Community Builder

How I Got My Start

It all started at a school-wide assembly at George Washington Elementary in Mount Clemens, Michigan. As my fourth-grade class shuffled into the auditorium, I had no idea that the next hour would completely transform my life.

The man on stage had so much energy and the words that flowed from his mouth made me feel like I could leap tall buildings in a single bound. He hadn't yet made a name for himself, but today he's known by audiences all over the world as Miss Mamie Brown's baby boy—none other than Les Brown.

As I sat in the audience, I thought to myself, "I want to make people feel like this. I want to be a speaker, too!" Then I went to lunch and thought no more about it. Although I had uncovered a piece of my calling that day, it would be another two decades before I cashed my first check as a professional speaker.

Even though I wasn't purposely focused on the goal I set as a nine-year-old, my life continued to prepare me for it. My high school teacher, Mr. Farago, insisted that we attend Toastmasters even though we weren't legally old enough to join. My senior year, I ranked sixth in the nation in extemporaneous speaking in a co-curricular club called Business Professionals of America. I knew I wanted to serve people from the stage, but I had no idea what I would talk about. Back then, all of the speakers I heard were highly accomplished or had overcome some insurmountable challenge. That wasn't my life—at least not yet. But whenever the opportunity to speak came, I took it.

Over the next 15 years, I accepted countless unpaid invitations to speak at career days, community events, and workshops, and I even emceed fashion shows. Most notably, I delivered the commencement address at my old high school the year my little brother graduated and had the honor of introducing the late Maya Angelou to a standing-room-only arena crowd at Central Michigan University. I still didn't know my "niche," but I took every opportunity to develop my gift.

When I was laid off from my job as a global communications and branding manager in 2009, my full-fledged speaking career began. I landed an opportunity with Monster's Making it Count program the same year, delivering high school assemblies to help students across the nation succeed in high school and beyond. It was a full-circle moment as young people waited in line to tell me how I made them feel like they could do anything—often with tears in their eyes as they shared challenging details about their lives.

I had achieved my fourth-grade goal.

I also joined the training team for a global consulting company that kept me working two weeks out of the month. That was a perfect frequency for me because it gave me time to grow my newly hatched professional development company, Epiphany Institute. I was personally mentored by the owner of the company who held nothing back when it came to sharing his secrets for successful facilitation and curriculum development. At the end of each day he'd have a laundry list of feedback for me. I couldn't get down on myself when he pointed out an area of improvement or if I felt like he expected too much of me. He knew what I was capable of and pushed me harder than any of the other trainers. I also had to remember that it wasn't about giving a dazzling performance—it was all about helping the participants to connect with the concepts we were teaching in a way that changed their lives.

One thing I quickly realized is that although I enjoy traveling, I am NOT a road warrior. Catching flights every week and dealing with delays and time zone changes while living out of a suitcase is not my cup of tea. I also realized that I get bored delivering the same content day in and day out—even though every audience is unique. As I grew Epiphany Institute, I intentionally developed my business model so that I had variety in my work and plenty of time at home with my son, which was critical to me as a single mother.

Along with keynotes and corporate training, I round out Epiphany Institute's offerings with a year-long program for authors, experts, consultants, and emerging speakers called Platform for Purpose; online course sales; and hosting my own workshops close to home. I don't like the details of planning big events, so intimate intensives where attendees get more one-on-one attention are my specialty. I also realized that I find just as much joy in equipping other experts to share their message as I do in taking the platform myself.

As you build your speaking career, remember that there isn't one model for success. You can shape your efforts around what you're good at, what you most enjoy, and the life you want instead of simply doing what you see others do.

My Advice to Aspiring Professional Speakers
Speak for impact, not applause.
I get it. You want to do a great job. No one accepts a speaking engagement thinking to themselves, "I wonder if I can put my

audience to sleep." But it's easy to take that desire too far, shifting the focus to yourself instead of keeping it on your audience.

Even after nearly 30 years of speaking, I still get nervous because I never take the honor and responsibility of the platform for granted. But if you find yourself dealing with debilitating levels of stage fright, it's likely that the people pleaser in you is kicking in.

What's the difference between wanting to do a good job and wanting to impress people? Wanting to do a good job is focused on serving your audience. Wanting to impress them is about serving your own ego.

If you want to be a great speaker, think about being B.A.D.:

B – Better: How do you want your audience to be better because they heard from you?

A – Action: What action can you challenge your audience to take related to your message?

D – Decision: What decision can you encourage them to make that will lead to personal transformation?

Answering these questions effectively requires you to get to know your audience. Here are a few additional questions to ponder:

- What challenges do they routinely face related to your message?
- What keeps them from being able to solve these problems on their own?
- What are their fears related to the change you wish to inspire? What are their aspirations?

- What does their negative self-talk sound like related to this area?
- What mental shift is necessary?

I encourage you to focus on honing your craft, discovering techniques to communicate your message more effectively. But more important, I urge you to put yourself in the place of your audience by getting clear on what you want for them *and what they need from you* before you script a single line of your speech.

Imagine running into someone who was in your audience several years after they heard you. Would you rather they go on and on about how charismatic you were on stage, or would you want to hear how your presentation changed their life?

Although social media provides people with vehicles to share their messages more broadly, we have a very unique opportunity as speakers. Being able to look into the eyes of our audience as our words connect to their heads and hearts is an experience that streaming video and podcasts will never replace.

Congratulations on your decision to pick up the microphone and change the world! If you need me, I'm here for you.

ABOUT ISHA

Whether she's hosting satellite broadcasts with Oscar-winning actress Hilary Swank, giving career advice in magazines like *Ebony* and *Cosmo*, or landing in the top three percent of finalists for a show on the Oprah Winfrey Network, Isha's mission is to help you build the career of your dreams. Isha is the founder of Epiphany Institute where she specializes in helping coaches, consultants, authors, and other experts build their platforms and personal brands so they can make a bigger impact on the world. She's the author of personal branding primer, *5 Rules to Win Being You*, and the force behind the book, *On Purpose: Practical Strategies to Live Your Best Life*.

Tried by fire, Isha operates with resilience birthed from being a teenage mother on welfare, corporate layoffs, and a bout with homelessness after a failed business venture. Determined to find purpose in her struggles, Isha founded Startup Life Support in 2017 to help entrepreneurs overcome the fear, frustration, and isolation of starting a business.

When you work with Isha, it's like hiring three experts in one—a certified life and corporate coach, business strategist, and a seasoned PR pro who served as a global communications and branding manager for one of the world's largest corporations.

Isha earned a degree in Broadcast and Cinematic Arts from Central Michigan University. She's a member of Alpha Kappa Alpha Sorority, Inc. and a volunteer with Kauffman Foundation's 1 Million Cups initiative.

A Michigan native, Isha lives in the Phoenix area and enjoys Netflix binges with her adult son, Deon. You can connect with Isha on your favorite social media networks and subscribe to her podcasts, *Clear Talk* and *On Purpose with Isha Cogborn* wherever you listen.

LESSONS LEARNED FROM ISHA

What caught your attention? What are your takeaways?

9
Become an Expert in at Least One Thing
By TeLISA DAUGHTRY
Serial Social Entrepreneur | Impact Investor | International Keynote Speaker

How I Got My Start

My first professional speaking events came via pitching competitions as an entrepreneur. I had to learn how to create and craft a compelling story to better promote my business and product to acquire money, partners, press, and customers. My ability to do this helped me to scale my business with 600+ partners in just one year with NO EXPERIENCE and gain visibility through incredible press and media outlets.

Having this experience helped me become a sought-after speaker speaking on topics regarding entrepreneurship, scaling businesses, pitching, and securing and leveraging media and press for startups.

In 2016, I started to take my speaking engagements seriously, and out the gate, it landed me my first video interview with **Entrepreneur.com;** and speaking engagements at the **White House, United Nations General Assembly, SXSW,** and **Grace Hopper Celebration**. By 2017 I had spoken at over **100+ events**, conferences, corporate events, workshops, and interviews. Plus, I have been paid 60% of the time! Speaking had been my side hustle to my full-time role as founder of my tech startup **FlyTechnista,** but as of today, I am 80% financially sustained just by my speaking career alone! I have achieved this WITHOUT submitting any calls for proposals to speak; 3% of my speaker requests come through my website, 42% are through referrals and word-of-mouth, and 55% are through my social media and sharing relevant content.

Being knowledgeable in an area of expertise with proven experience and credibility helped me establish myself as a speaker. It also provided me with the opportunity to secure more notable speaking engagements and the ability to be compensated for my words and knowledge.

My Advice to Aspiring Professional Speakers
The greatest piece of advice that I offer aspiring speakers is to BECOME AN EXPERT in at least one thing! This should be something that you have significant experience in, know in great depth, and can explain to someone in a clear and simplified way; this is what makes you sought-after and valuable.

The ability to become a paid speaker comes from two things:
1. Your ability to add value to people's businesses or lives by helping them to simplify a process, solve a problem, or provide a solution.
2. Your ability to provide in-depth and unique insight.

ABOUT TeLISA

TeLisa Daughtry is an award-winning diversity and tech advocate, serial social entrepreneur, impact investor, author, multi-disciplined creative, technologist, and disruptor! She is the founder and CTO of FlyTechnista and founder of STEEAMnista; both initiatives were in partnership with the White House in 2016. She is also the founder of and an impact investor at FemX Ventures. She is the author of the e-book *Learn, Lead, Launch: A FlyTechnista's Guide to Tech FLY & Hustle FLY.*

In 2018, she was named 50 Most Influential Women Entrepreneurs in New York City by My Boss Tribe. In 2017, she was an honoree and recipient of an ACT4 Award, recognized for her achievements in technology and advocacy for diversity; a Finalist for Code/Interactive: Diversity in Tech Awards; listed on MIC's 1,000 Women in Tech and Science Speakers; and named Top 50 Visionary Women in Tech to Watch in 2017 by *Innov8tiv Magazine*. In 2016, she was recognized as a Changemaker for Innovation & Entrepreneurship by the United State of Women.

As an international keynote speaker, she has spoken at venues such as The White House, United Nations General Assembly, Anita Borg/Grace Hopper, SXSW Edu, Google Women Techmakers, American Heart Association, DevTO, Harvard University, Wellesley College as well as several conferences, corporate events, and institutions and has been featured on television, radio, and in publications such as *Entrepreneur*, Fox News, *Black Enterprise*,

Cheddar TV, CNN, CBS Radio, Salon, "Good Day New York," WE Rule, Bustle, BOLD, SWAAY, and more.

LESSONS LEARNED FROM TeLISA
What caught your attention? What are your takeaways?

10
Done is Better Than Perfect ... Start With the "Why"
By GLYNIS DEVINE
Bilingual Keynote Speaker | Emcee | Executive Facilitator | Transformational Retreat Leader

How I Got My Start

All spontaneous decisions I've made in my life, when analyzed, were anything but "spontaneous."

In my "Squeeze the Day!" keynote, it can sound like my career paradigm shifted sitting in a pool of tears on the bathroom floor. Upon further analysis many years later, I realize that many individual moments led to that crescendo.

I started my 28-year career in the cosmetic industry at the age of 20. Over those 28 years, I amassed incredible success; I'd earned the use of a company car (yes, pink)—for free—for fourteen years, had earned more diamond rings than I had fingers to wear them on, and was recognized as #5 out of 30,000 sales professionals. My claim to fame, for that era of my career, is that I'd sold half a million dollars' worth of lipstick.

To put that into perspective, if you put half a million dollars' worth of lipstick end to end (try it with any two in your purse) it adds up to the height of the CN Tower (in Canada where I live) four and a half times, or if you're an American, it adds up to the height of the Empire State Building ... FIVE and a half times—that's a LOT of kisses!!

So, imagine my surprise when I looked in the mirror one morning and realized I was miserable. It wasn't that I hadn't been blessed in that career—I had! It wasn't that I wasn't grateful—I was! It wasn't that I didn't love my clients and the women in my organization—I did! It was that I didn't feel I was doing what I was "meant" to do. That's the feeling I felt that landed me in a pool of tears on the bathroom floor the morning my speaking business rose like a phoenix.

The process I went through to find my "why" in life is what I speak on today.

Why speaking?

Five months before that fateful breakdown on my bathroom floor, one of my colleagues asked me what my goals were for the new year. I whipped off four things I was passionate about achieving. I went on to rhyme off why I wanted to achieve each one—and thought it was curious that ALL of them put me in a position on-stage at various events—to mentor to aspiring directors. THAT should have been my sign that I'd one day make my living speaking.

Speaking, mentoring, and helping someone to the next level all align with my currencies—why I do what I do.

Now, one of the first exercises I do with participants of Your Soul Journey is a "life scan"—backwards. Starting with this year, write down all the highlights of your life. Then, look for patterns of what "juices" you.

My "spontaneous" decision to leave my 28-year career and start a speaking business … was 28 years in the making!

My Advice to Aspiring Professional Speakers
Today, as a Purpose Expert, I work with organizations and leaders who want to figure out why they do what they do so they can do what they do more effectively.

My advice to aspiring and developing speakers, therefore, is… start with the "why."

CAVEAT: I'm a mom of three; the following business advice mirrors my mantra for parenting … *"do what I say not what I did!"*

I've been in business for 10 years as a professional (paid) speaker, and I'm only NOW doing the fundamental work that I'm suggesting you do *before* you start. That said, my second (unsolicited) piece of business advice is to not wait for everything to be perfect before you start. My (other) mantra is *"Done is better than perfect, any day!"*

Here, let's talk about my foremost piece of business advice … laying the groundwork or what I call "setting yourself up for success."

I've been an entrepreneur since the age of 20. I started self-employment as a contractor with a direct sales organization in the cosmetic industry. That career spanned 28 years, and my claim to fame was that I sold half a million dollars' worth of lipstick and earned a few pink cars.

What I took for granted as an entrepreneur affiliated with a multi-national company was the infrastructure that the direct sales company had built when it started. When I left that career and started my own solopreneurship, I didn't do the same due diligence in my speaking business that the cosmetic company had done.

That company had …
- a vision statement
- a mission statement
- an "ideal client" avatar
- a value offering and expectation
- a *"why me"* statement

- a value proposition for deliverables
- list of currencies accepted
- a product line
- research and development
- a sales cycle strategy
- a marketing strategy
- a social media strategy
- a training manual

I didn't have ANY of that when I started speaking professionally.

There are two primary approaches entrepreneurs take when starting a business. One is the *Field of Dreams* version: *"if you build it, they will come,"* which refers to setting up the infrastructure, strategy, and planning ahead of time.

The second is "on the fly" referring to designing, building, delivering, and modifying as you go.

The benefit of the first approach is that you have an intentional, aligned plan. The drawback can be that you suffer paralysis by analysis and never quite get off the ground because you're waiting to have the "perfect system."

The benefit of the second approach is that you can start speaking right away and morph and grow your business in time—and with the experience and influence of mentors. The drawback of this approach is that your success can feel intermittent and accidental. In hindsight, a blend of both may have been a more lucrative strategy.

My results might have been less "experimental" or "accidental" and more "intentional" and "strategic" had I taken the time to prepare for success in my speaking business. That stated, I didn't have that luxury. I had left a career with which I'd paid the mortgage to start a new speaking career where I had no plan, no clients, and no contacts.

At the very beginning, I had started to strategize. I got some of the fundamentals in place (a website, business cards, etcetera) then ran out of money. I quickly started contracting for a training company, teaching its material for the company and making significantly less than what I make now teaching my own intellectual property (IP).

To make enough money to pay my mortgage with the training company for which I contracted, I had to speak in five cities five consecutive days for three weeks out of every month. I didn't make much money. The upside was … because I was speaking so often, I got REALLY good at speaking. I told my stories (relevant storytelling tied to strategies that can be applied immediately that net positive outcomes is the most successful way to speak in this era) 300+ times over 24 months; therefore, my stories—and how I delivered them— got better and better.

So, while I didn't have a directional "blueprint," accidental speaking netted one primary benefit; I got good at my craft.

IF, however, I had had the luxury of time (and income to sustain me for a while) to *plan* my speaker success, I'd have taken the time to build my blueprint.

Assuming you are far smarter (and richer) than was I starting out … let's unpack at least the first few components of the blueprint process for a successful speaking business.

A vision statement

Your vision statement is what you GET out of having your speaker business. It's an inward-facing statement that you don't share with your clients. It's *your* why.

To help you start your list, here are some of the reasons I do what I do. My speaking business lets me:

- do something I love to do
- do something I'm good at
- make good money
- do what I think I'm meant to do
- do something that helps people
- perform
- feel admired
- travel to exotic places
- hang out with people who *want* to grow and develop
- (try to) provoke positive change

In short, it's what I GET OUT of my speaking business.

A mission statement

Your mission statement is what you GIVE to others through your speaking business. It's an outward-facing statement that you share with your clients on your website, marketing material, etcetera. It completes the statement "When you work with me, you can expect to arrive at x result."

Your mission statement can answer the following:

I work with _____ (whom)

To do _____ (what)

So they can _____ (result)

I have a different one for each of my two primary types of clients—one for organizations and one for individuals (leaders).

"I work with organizations who invest in their female leaders so they can grow exponentially."

"I work with female leaders who want more—more time, more balance, more joy, and more fun—so they can squeeze the best out of life!"

Values offered and expected
Values, quite simply, are what's important to you. I designed a list of values I deem important if you want to work with me AND what values I look for in someone with whom I want to work.

Clients who choose to work with me appreciate that I value
- ethical practices
- honest and respectful communication
- reliable research
- compassionate conversations
- engaging experiences

Companies that I choose to work with are organizations that
- are profit-making
- have healthy vision and mission
- want and value gender balanced leadership
- build up their people
- strive for win-win solutions
- treat their employees respectfully
- are inclusive
- have sustainable, eco-friendly products/services
- are socially responsible and give back to the community

"Why me?"

Marketers who I've sought out for help developing my speaking business always ask, *"Why you? Why should your client work with YOU instead of your competition?"*

My answer, too often, was tears that welled up in my eyes, shrugging shoulders, and an *"I suck!"* pathetic look on my face.

It's taken me 10 years to realize that it's no ONE thing that makes each of us unique. It's like the winning recipe for cremes brûlée (my favorite dessert). While it's only three ingredients, generally, it's how, when, and how much of each are mixed together that makes it meh or mouth-watering.

The ingredients that combine to make me unique are
- I love learning;
- I have a lot of different interests;
- I know a lot of people with different interests;
- I research well—and thoroughly;
- I'm dogged about finding a solution;
- I get a kick out of connecting people I know and trust;
- I invest time in understanding the problem they're hiring me to solve;
- I communicate with compassion;
- I celebrate success;
- I do what I say I'm going to do (this isn't as common as you think); and
- I set up people for success.

You'll want to write a list of yours. Then, ask a friend—or two—for their input. My friend Corey said she'd add "charismatic" and "eternally optimistic." So, I added those to my list, too.

I liked doing this section.

An "ideal client" avatar
When you are starting out, you may not (yet) have any clients. So, this may be more of a wish list.

In time, you'll get to know who "juices" you when you work with them. Keep in mind that your decision-maker is who pays you. The participants are the end-users (the audience). Sometimes they're the same; often they're not. Design an avatar for your ideal client (decision-maker). Many speakers name their avatars; mine is named Patricia.

Here are some generic criteria to consider for your list. I work with decision-makers who
- pay their bills joyfully and on time;
- invest in their people—have a professional development strategy;
- respect my expertise;
- are interested in solutions; and
- work with, not against, me.

You may also want to consider
- the size of the organization
- type of industry
- types of problems they solve
- the client they serve

If your decision-maker is not the same person as your participant, you'll want to design a different avatar for your participant; mine is named Maria. You'll want to market differently to Maria than to Patricia because their motives are different.

A value proposition

This is the RESULT of what your menu items do. It's a laundry list of the problems you solve. You'll have a different value proposition for each solution you offer. I teach professional development programs, and I also run a transformational retreat for women leaders. I developed a statement (that includes a list of outcomes) for *each*.

For example, organizations who work with me and apply my strategies:

- reduce conflict
- increase communication
- improve collaboration
- stress less
- empower their leaders
- shift mindsets

Shelle Rose Charvet, an international speaker, Neuro-linguistic Programming (NLP) expert, and author of *Words that Change Minds: The 14 Patterns for Mastering the Language of Influence* reminded me to consider "towards" (improve performance) and "away from" (reduce stress) outcomes.

In contrast, female leaders who come away on our transformational retreats report leaving with

- serenity
- clarity
- a better sense of who they are and for what they are searching
- direction
- renewed vitality and hope
- tools to communicate more effectively
- a greater sense of self confidence

Currencies

As I'm writing this, ABBA's song, "Money, Money, Money" is blaring in my ears! Money is NOT most entrepreneurs' primary currency.

I remember one of the first speakers from whom I learned was Linda Edgecombe, CSP (Certified Speaking Professional). She said, "I'll work for anything from a bottle of Shiraz to full fee—it all depends."

Over the years, I've also heard speakers defend "fee integrity"—the notion that all clients should pay the exact same amount for the same message/program regardless of variables.

I'm with Linda. I've accepted $500 for speaking in the Bahamas at a world-class resort for me and my husband. I'd accept nothing short of full fee to work in Thunder Bay in February (read REALLY cold and complicated travel) and my currency for working in Saudi over Thanksgiving weekend and missing pumpkin pie and family was $10,000.

So clearly, money is not one of my "fixed" currencies. It's also not my primary currency. Some of my currencies are
- travelling to exotic (read WARM; I'm Canadian) places
- whether I can take family or friends or visit family or friends while I'm there
- speaking in cool venues, a.k.a. bragging rights
- admiration—I'm finally okay with admitting this
- potential for future business
- stimulating conversations
- who else is speaking from whom I can learn and with whom I can hang out

For clues to what some of your currencies are you can refer back to your vision statement.

A product line

There is a number of ways for us to share our intellectual property (IP). Consider the following avenues and which are a fit for your message, then decide how your clients are going to "consume" your IP. You can consider

- keynotes
- workshops
- webinars
- online courses
- a book
- a retreat
- seminars
- emceeing

By the time you get to this point, you have a strong foundation. From here, the other steps will start to fall into place.

While there is a myriad of components to a successful speaking career that require a specific skill set—delivery techniques, processes and systems, etcetera, etcetera—I believe that all that is useless if you don't first set up your foundation.

Carve out a *limited* amount of uninterrupted time to do the above-mentioned steps; I call them "mind" work.

Knowing your "why" will make you more likely to find your "way" to a successful, gratifying career with clients who refer other like-minded clients to you.

That stated, don't spend so much time setting up your foundation that paralysis sets in; get 'er done—quickly! Then, get speaking. Remember that "done" IS better than "perfect;" you'll re-invent yourself often. We all do.

There are as many speaking business models as there are speakers in the world. Start with what works for you, and be open to grow and develop.

And lastly—have fun and enjoy the ride!

ABOUT GLYNIS

Chief Juicer, Glynis E. Devine works with female leaders who want to squeeze the best out of life!

The wisdom she shares is gleaned from 25 years leading a top sales team in the cosmetics industry as a Senior Director cosmetics industry as a Senior Director. She's sold more than a half million dollars' worth of lipstick.

Organizations hire Glynis to develop their female leaders so they can grow exponentially.
Glynis is the founder of the SHE-Suite movement and leader of Your Soul Journey, a women's transformational retreat in Portugal.

Glynis has …
- led 650+ sessions in French and English
- trained female leaders in Saudi Arabia for Vision 2030
- held the position of Ethics Chair for the Canadian Association of Professional Speakers

Glynis is a wife, mom of three, a coffee and shoe addict, and a dancing fool.

www.glynisedevine.com
www.yoursouljourneyretreat.com/portugal
514.298.6529

LESSONS LEARNED FROM GLYNIS

What caught your attention? What are your takeaways?

SECTION 1 ACTION PLAN

Based on what you learned from the contributors in this section, what action will you take?

SECTION 2

11
People Want to Hear Your Struggles Along With Your Triumphs
By ELIZABETH DILLON
Motivational Speaker | Revolutionary Change Agent | Navy Wife

How I Got My Start

I was in the middle of a hectic senior year of college that entailed full-time classes, volunteering, and working. I had led our Student Chapter of Society of Human Resource Management (SHRM) in philanthropic initiatives and knew that HR was where I was supposed to be. I wanted to make a difference in the world and be there for my future employees. One night, my husband I were home, deciding on dinner, when I heard a car accident happen outside. I lifted the blinds to see a woman screaming in the road and a man lying face down on the pavement. I asked my husband if I should help and ran out the door before he could even respond. I immediately leapt into action and told two women to stop traffic so that I could start first aid and CPR. Once the ladies had ensured we were safe, I got down on my hands and knees and told the gentleman that he had been in an accident and asked if he could hear me. I repeated it and still no response. I went to check for a pulse and immediately could feel the adrenaline pumping through my veins. I could hear my own heartbeat in my head and knew that I had to calm down or I wouldn't be able to decipher if he had a heartbeat, too. I asked one of the women who stopped traffic to double-check for a pulse. This was a critical moment in this man's life. We needed to make sure not to move him if he's breathing so as to not cause spinal injury. If he was not breathing, then we would have had to turn him over and immediately start compressions. The woman said she felt a faint pulse. I knew in my core that wasn't true but wanted to be absolutely certain of my next move. The other women said she didn't feel a pulse. I was about to flip him over and start compressions when an officer came running up. I let him know there was not a pulse and he would have to start compressions immediately. As I stepped back, I just kept praying for God to save this man—not just for his family but for the woman who had hit him as well. She was around 19 and was just starting her life in the medical field. As hard as I prayed, they eventually brought out a white sheet, and I sobbed uncontrollably.

As the days went by and the shock wore off, I realized that situation taught me more than I ever could have imagined. I realized that when someone's life was on the line that I would go into action. He was completely different than me. He was a different gender, race, and generation from myself. I learned in that time of self-reflection that I was a leader and that I wouldn't let anything get in my way when it comes to helping people.

I started in my HR profession with purpose and passion. I got involved with the professional chapter in my area called Michiana SHRM. Within two years, I had moved into the vice president's position. My president at the time said that she wanted to hear a presentation about Millennials that was actually given by a Millennial. I stepped up to the challenge, but I had a fear of public speaking. With my profound new strength to lead and advocate, I thought this would be a great time to overcome my fear and create further impact in my community.

Kruggel Lawton CPAs provided their data that they had compiled on Millennials for my presentation. I compiled HR theories that I had learned in college while utilizing people's stories and experiences. I shared an example about myself and my family's struggles during the presentation as well. My husband and I had six jobs between the two of us, and we were both Millennials. Not only that, but my grandmother had Stage IV Metastatic Breast Cancer, and I was helping to care for her while preparing for this presentation. I was terrified when I got on stage, but by the time I was finished, it felt like my soul was on fire. I had found my true calling to supplement my passion so that I could fulfill my purpose in life. I loved teaching, engaging, sharing, and bonding with my audience. I told my grandmother that this would be where my future would lie. Her sight was failing, but she could hear the determination in my voice. I went to church with her and got to share my story. Afterwards, she said that she, too, believed that I would do well in this profession.

I've continued giving presentations and advocating for employees. Sharing my experiences along with others and showing data have impacted the professionals in my region. They are starting to reconsider programs, policies, and medical benefits to better assist the employees and their needs.

My Advice to Aspiring Professional Speakers
First and foremost, be confident and authentic. My public speaking mentors and I have spoken on the importance of connecting with your audience. There have been studies done that show people want to hear stories and know that you can relate to them. Most of my feedback from the first few presentations were that people wanted to hear my struggles along with my triumphs. Receiving constructive feedback allows for you to make incremental changes to evolve your presentation.

Networking is crucial for business professionals and public speakers. Be sure to connect with everyone and find mentors! I connected with Bridgett McGowen after one of her speaking engagements. She was so engaging and passionate that I knew we had to connect. While being mentored by Bridgett and others, they all said that you need to be consistent on price!

ABOUT ELIZABETH

Elizabeth formerly worked for a human resources information system (HRIS) company where she trained clients on how to fully utilize the system. With her public speaking passion growing, she created a consulting company called Revolutionary HR where she is CEO, Lead Consultant, and Public Speaker. In her free time, she has done pro bono résumé, interview, and LinkedIn consulting for veterans and the unemployed.

She is currently the Michiana SHRM vice president of membership and is working her way up to president in the future. Starting in 2020, Beth will be working for the HR Indiana State Council. They have created a position that will allow her to work with the Membership and Workforce Readiness Committee. Beth will be traveling throughout the state to educate others on the HR Indiana and SHRM Foundation's initiative to get veterans reintegrate back into the civilian workforce.

LESSONS LEARNED FROM ELIZABETH

What caught your attention? What are your takeaways?

12
Market Yourself: Do Not Keep Yourself a Secret
By MONA DIXON
International Motivational Speaker | Fundraiser | Coach

How I Got My Start

When I was 16 years old, my Boys & Girls Club staff asked me if I wanted to participate in a Youth of the Year competition. The Youth of the Year Award is the highest award that a Club member can receive, and you compete against other Youth of the Year contenders from other Clubs with a speech on what the Club means to you, you have one-on-one interviews with the judges, and you have panel interviews. I hesitated at first because he told me that I would have to share my story of homelessness. However, he then revealed to me that at every level that I won, I could receive scholarship money for college. The rest was history! I won locally, on the state level, at the regional level, and then I became the National Youth of the Year (NYOY) for Boys & Girls Clubs of America in 2010, winning over $100,000 in scholarships!

While I was the NYOY, I was the youth spokesperson for a year, representing over 4.2 million youth from all over the world! When I first started speaking, I never thought it would turn into a career until people from the audiences started coming up to me, asking how much I charged! This was shocking and caught me off guard! I first started speaking for free, then I increased to a small amount from $100 to $250. Then it went up to $500, then $1,000 and so on.... Eventually, I knew that I had to get an LLC. However, for the first seven years, I just relied on word of mouth referrals or when people would hear me speak and then ask me to speak at their events as well. It was not until a couple of years ago that I started to actually market myself and get more speaking engagements.

My Advice to Aspiring Professional Speakers

The one most important piece of advice that I have for aspiring professional speakers, especially my students who are just kick-starting their speaking platforms, is to understand that sales and marketing are two very important skills to learn in the speaking business. Before you start to market yourself, ask yourself what you are an expert in. What do you know a lot about and are very passionate about? This topic is what you should speak on!

The next step is to determine what kind of value you can bring to others based on that topic. Can you teach people how to overcome obstacles? Can you teach people to live a healthier life? Can you teach people how to grow their social media following with organic reach? Once you decide what you are an expert in and what value you can provide, then you can begin to market yourself. Without marketing, your speaking engagements will trickle in slowly. Marketing allows you to let people know that you exist and that you can provide value to your target market by providing the solution to their problems or needs. Marketing is not just announcing your services but strategically addressing pain points and offering yourself as a solution. There are many ways to market yourself and gain exposure, so research them and do not put all of your eggs in one basket! Diversify your marketing strategy.

Next, once you have your presentations and programs together, you can now start to sell them. How much should you charge to give a presentation? Don't value yourself too low, and make sure you research your competition and see how much they charge. You don't want to undercut them, but you do want to show that you can provide more value than they can! Then once you land the presentation gig, determine beforehand if you can sell something at the event, whether it's your book or coaching packages. It's great to know this beforehand because you can work on how you are going to sell your products or services to the audience. You can also ask for the audience to not keep you a secret and to let others know about you just in case they need a speaker down the line.

ABOUT MONA

Mona and her family lived on the streets and moved from one homeless shelter to another until she was the age of 13. A few short years later she was honored by President Obama in the Oval Office.

After receiving her coveted Boys & Girls Clubs of America National Youth of the Year Award, Mona was appointed by President Obama to serve as the youngest member of a U.S. Presidential Community Service Committee alongside four other distinguished individuals.

At 18, Mona was also named by *Essence Magazine* one of the Most Influential Black Women alongside Oprah Winfrey and Michelle Obama. This has all led to her being awarded over $100,000 in scholarships, sharing the stage with "A" list celebrities, being featured in the national media, and starring in a national campaign commercial with Mark Wahlberg.

Mona, at 27, is currently pursuing her doctoral degree in Organizational Leadership and empowering others while speaking for corporate companies, schools, youth organizations, fundraisers, graduations, parent organizations, and homeless shelters.

LESSONS LEARNED FROM MONA
What caught your attention? What are your takeaways?

13
Learn the Ropes and Hone Your Skills
By PRINCE HARRISON EHIMIYEN
Chairman, Prince Harrison Ehimiyen Foundation Board of Directors

How I Got My Start

By virtue of your existence and interaction with the social environment, you are bound to communicate with two or more people at one point or the other. This is because you live in a society where advancements are plentiful and communication is instantaneous. You must consistently and consciously drive effective communication as aspiring leaders so that if you cannot convince them, you should, at least, be able to confuse them.

As would-be leaders, it is important for you to know very early that the art of communication is the language of leadership. I knew very early in life that the singular powerful force available to humanity is words. We can choose to use this force constructively with words of encouragement or destructively with words of despair. I also knew words have power and energy with the ability to heal, to help, to hurt, to harm, to humiliate, and to humble depending on how they were communicated.

I recalled vividly how I honed my public speaking skills in the year 2000 after my Senior Secondary School when, as a gateman in Continental Group of Schools, Benin City, Edo State, Nigeria, I volunteered to teach without any promptings nor remuneration. Upon realizing that the school was deficient in certain subjects, including government, I knew I had speaking potential inherent in me. But I needed to work on my public speaking style, sharpness, clarity, and emotions to affect and move my audience. "This is the opportunity I have been waiting for," I said to myself.

I made the constant effort and took practical steps alongside the advantage of every available opportunity to practice and develop my communication skills (communication is the very core of our society; that is what makes us human), for I knew the occasion and opportunity will arise, then it will be needed.

When I later became the Principal of Magdon Comprehensive College, still in Benin City, Edo State, I had removed most of the inhibition to public speaking and realized that people always listened to me with rapt attention whenever the opportunity presents itself for me to talk to or address them.

In 2009, when I became University of Benin Students' Union Government President and a youth pastor in my local church, my public speaking skills had become so developed and sharpened that people started calling me an orator, and with time, I started getting guest speaker invitations to various speaking engagements.

Although many persons have said to me, "Harrison, public speaking comes naturally for you." But what they have all failed to know is that I am a very shy person. What I lack in boldness, I make up for with the abundance of the substance in the message I intend to communicate to my audience, and this, to a large extent, immediately masked the shyness when I am handed the microphone or when I mount the podium.

It was the American author and motivational speaker Zig Ziglar who said "There is no elevator to success, you have to take the stairs." This is true when you realize that half the world is composed of people who have something to say and can't say it and the other half who have nothing to say and keep on saying it. Miscommunication is the number one cause of all problems from family, to the relationship, to leadership, to an organization, to society because the sensitivity of men is built on words. Effective communication is the bridge to other people. Without it, there is nothing. It is all huff and puff.

My Advice to Aspiring Professional Speakers

Effective communication is a skill that you can learn. It is like riding a bicycle or typing a manuscript. If you are willing to work at it, you can rapidly improve on the quality of your speech. Therefore, my most important piece of advice to aspiring professional speakers is learn the ropes and hone your skills by equipping yourself with the necessary knowledge and network to build a successful career and create an impact in the world.

ABOUT PRINCE HARRISON

Prince Harrison, EHIMIYEN, was born on October 31, 1981 into the family of Mr. and Mrs. Robinson Idaheloise Ehimiyen and Grace Izah in Iuleha, Uzebba, Owan West Local Government Area, Edo State.

Prince Harrison received his pre-primary education at Stella Marries Nursery School, Ashaka, Delta State and his primary education at Ogene Primary School, Ashaka Delta State, Ohia Primary School in Owan West, Edo State, respectively, before proceeding to the famous Uzebba Grammar School, Uzebba, Uselu Secondary School, Uselu and Iuleha Grammar School all in Edo State for his secondary education.

His passion and desire to develop his ability to engage in political activities with a greater understanding of the processes involved and gaining practical knowledge on critical thinking and political analytical skills made him study political science and public administration during his first degree at the prestigious University of Benin, Benin City, Edo State, Nigeria having previously earned a Diploma in Law, from the same University.

In search for more knowledge, he enrolled for two years in an International Relations Master of Science program, studying variety of courses ranging from policy analysis to policy advocacy. Currently, he is a PhD student at the University of Benin, Benin City, Edo State, Nigeria.

Upon completion of his M.Sc. program, he was employed as a graduate assistant in the Department of Political Science and Public Administration in University of Benin. Thereafter, he was promoted to an assistant lecturer and recently promoted to Lecturer 2.

In November 2015, while enjoying an illustrious career as an assistant lecturer and as a PhD student in the same university, a national assignment to serve as principal private secretary to Nigeria's Honorable Minister of State, Petroleum Resources from Dr. Emmanuel Ibe Kachikwu, who then was the Group Managing Director, Nigeria National Petroleum Corporation, came calling. He obeyed. He has carried-on his duties and responsibilities with precision, commitment, and excellence to the admiration of Nigerians.

In January 2016, he founded the renowned Prince Harrison Ehimiyen Foundation, one of the leading charitable foundations in Nigeria dedicated to facilitating innovations for youths, underprivileged, and vulnerable through its various innovative social services, skills acquisition, empowerment programs, leadership trainings, and advocacy campaigns.

In 2009, Prince Harrison was a participant at the United States of America Students' Leadership (SUSI) and Community Development Training organized by former President Barack Obama in conjunction with Spring Field International and Arkansas State University.

Prince Harrison, one of the shrewdest and most compelling figures who is a youth in Nigeria political space today, ascending from obscurity to a circle or celebrity, to his teeming admirers, has done remarkably well given the circumstances he found himself.

In 2018, Prince Harrison was a participant at the International Human Resources Department Corporation (IHRDC) in Boston, Massachusetts where he earned a certificate after active participation in and successful completion of a four-day training in an executive workshop on value chain in the oil and gas sector in Nigeria. While in 2019, he was also awarded a certificate after participating in a professional development program on leadership communication at Harvard University Extension School, Cambridge, Massachusetts.

He has attended and spoken in several high-level local, regional, and international conferences, symposia, seminars, and workshops, including the famed Edo Youth Leadership Summit (EDYLeadS), and he is a recipient of over a dozen leadership, good governance, and humanitarian awards. Happily, he is married to Mrs. Rosemary Prince Harrison Ehimiyen. They are blessed with two lovely kids, Prince Harrison, Jr. and Princess Benison.

LESSONS LEARNED FROM PRINCE HARRISON

What caught your attention? What are your takeaways?

14
You Already Have What It Takes to Be Successful
By KLYN ELSBURY
Motivational Speaker | Hypnotist and NLP Coach | Best-Selling Author | Podcast Host

How I Got My Start

Klyn Elsbury's lungs are prone to infections because she naturally produces a thick sticky mucus that she can't cough out due to cystic fibrosis. It has destroyed her pancreas and requires her to take more than 30 pills a day just to digest food. The stress on her pancreas and years of malnutrition led to a month-long diabetic coma in 2001, and now she manages diabetes with daily insulin.

In 2018, she spent over 100 days on IV antibiotics accessed through a port that she had surgically implanted into her chest for immediate vein access.

Klyn dropped out of college (despite a 4.0 GPA) because she feared she would not live long enough to ever pay off her student loan debt, and at the age of 22, with only a few hundred dollars to her name, she found a career that capitalized on the essence of who she was—a super-connector.

Within the first two years after accepting the entry level job, she had a corner office, bought a house, and was solely in charge of all internal recruitment needs for a 26-million-dollar company. She was 22 years old.

As hospitalizations increased, work became tough—so tough, she was let go and decided to move to San Diego, California to be closer to the very drugs that were being made, hoping to save her own life. Yet in less than a year, she was exploring life on the lung transplant list.

Determined to avoid early death, with half of a lung, she honed physical and mental fortitude and passed licensure to become a certified Zumba Instructor. This bought her time.

When the drugs came on the market with a price tag of $259,000, she was denied coverage. Using her recruitment background, she ultimately wound up with a primetime slot with an Emmy-award winning correspondent of NBC's *Nightly News with Lester Holt*.

Once approved, the sky was the limit.

From her hospital bed, she began interviewing famous people who overcame incredible odds and wrote the best-selling book, *I AM ____: The Untold Story of Success*.

One night, while hanging out with several successful entrepreneurs, she was given the opportunity of a lifetime to keynote at an entrepreneurial conference with over 1,500 attendees. She would share the stage with Shep Gordon, Jocko Willinck, Ryan Holiday, and Darren Hardy. Later, she would find out she was the highest-rated speaker and was picked up by multiple bureaus.

Speaking all over the country opened up a new door of people who really wanted to understand her process behind surviving in the most difficult of times and wondered if they could take that process and apply it to business.

That was where the coaching program began. She completed her master's practitioner in neurolinguistic programming with a strong emphasis on hypnosis and has now worked with hundreds of business owners and sales representatives.

As popularity spread, she founded her podcast, Neuroscience for Sales Success.

My Advice to Aspiring Professional Speakers
I spent so much of my life living inside of hospitals that in 2016 when I wrote my book, I was determined to find out what the SECRET to success was.

I drained my savings into seminars, books, and invested in gurus. I figured if I wasn't going to live much longer, it was a great time to take what I thought was a risk financially.

And I implemented most of it. You see, I'm the kind of gal who, when given a to-do list, does it all and does it quickly. I thrive with checking things off my checklist.

And all their advice helped. Everyone contributed something magical to my experience whether it was how to speak on stage, get best-seller status, launch a profitable online course, coach execs and salespeople to overcome their issues and get back to closing—but there was a time when it wasn't sooo extra.

I looked at my website and cried.
and my pile of biz cards that I spent $100 on and hated so I never handed them out.
and my email campaigns.
and wardrobe.
and hair...

and the entire life I built only to realize I didn't recognize it.

You see what was missing was to be AUTHENTIC. To be ME.

To not capitalize every word because a copy writer tells you to.

To have a bit of color of your branding.

To curse like a sailor when something really needs to be said.

To have flaming red hair even though "agents don't like that."

Listen, you already have what it takes to be successful. You are the most successful resource there is. Sure, there's always room to improve on your systems and processes towards your dreams— that's when a coach can come in.

But the secret to success is already with you. I thought if I could just be more like my idols, I'd make it. What I slowly began to see as I got to know some of the world's best speakers, coaches, and podcasters was none of them was anyone else.

They were them.

It was in a span of one week I redid the site, dyed my hair red, threw all the clothes in my closet away, ditched the fancy copy, and just started talking to you as YOU, as ME, that my life finally fit together.

Be YOU.

There is nobody like you in this planet of like eight billion people.

You're the best we've got.

We need YOU to keep going because someone out there needs the gifts you bring this world. You're a very scarce commodity.

The more YOU you become, the better all the experts will be at helping you...

Connect with Klyn at www.missklyn.com

ABOUT KLYN

Born with cystic fibrosis, Klyn was told she wouldn't live past age 14 and has spent much of her life growing up inside hospitals, battling the disease.

Now, at 31, she helps entrepreneurs with teams stuck by their own expertise and fear or stubbornness by providing a science-based approach that immediately engages teams in management's vision because they don't need another pep-talk; they need a proven process.

Klyn's expertise has appeared in over 150 publications including a prime-time debut on NBC's *Nightly News with Lester Holt*, regularly keynotes for conferences and association events, and has a full coaching practice dedicated to helping entrepreneurs get "unstuck" leveraging hypnosis and neuro-linguistic programming.

LESSONS LEARNED FROM KLYN

What caught your attention? What are your takeaways?

15
Start with a Clear and Sincere Intention
By DAMON GIVEHAND
Yoga and Health Mindset Coach | Happiness Catalyst

How I Got My Start

In a nutshell, my start began with an intention and a little late by some standards. Outwardly, my intention was silent, but inwardly, my intention was as loud as could be. Around the age of 30, I decided and declared to myself that I WANT TO GROW. This was my intention. And the best way I could think to *really grow* was to face and embrace the biggest fear I knew I had that was holding me back. This BIG Fear was (drum roll please) … speaking to groups of people, large or small. My intention was clear, and at that moment, my request to the Universe was submitted. I gave it no further thought and left it up to Infinite Intelligence to do what it does best, which is to pull strings in our ultimate favor when we are CLEAR WITH OUR INTENTIONS.

Okay, you're probably thinking to yourself "SO HOW DID YOU GET STARTED?" I'm getting there, but first I want to give you a sense of how bad this fear was for me and why overcoming it was so important. So here it is…

During my first semester of undergraduate study as a freshman, I was enrolled in English 1101, heading into finals week with a high "B" average. Our culminating assignment for the term, which was worth 30% of our overall grade, was an oral presentation to the class. I was so terrified of giving my presentation that I accepted an "F," which brought my "B" down to a "D" average and landed me on academic probation. Apparently, *carpe diem* was NOT my motto at that time!

Fast forward 12 years. While enrolled in an evening graduate program for mathematics and education, one of my professors approached me about teaching at a local high school (where this professor taught during the day). This might have been just a few weeks after I declared my personal intention. I remember thinking, "WOW! What a perfect opportunity to face my fear in a *minimally threatening* environment." I didn't perceive speaking in front of younger people to be as intimidating as speaking as an authority in front of my peers; and talking about math wasn't scary at all since I was confident in my understanding of the subject matter and my students wanted to learn it from me. I couldn't imagine a better situation to be invited into to warm up to my fear.

Daily, I got the chance to practice speaking in front of groups of younger people, which really helped me become comfortable in this particular spotlight. And, at least a couple times per month, I'd participate in math department meetings where I would occasionally get other opportunities to practice speaking in front of small groups of other teachers, which allowed me to ease into feeling comfortable talking to my peers from the podium.

Over time, I figured out that it was never a FEAR OF PUBLIC SPEAKING that frightened me; it was a FEAR OF EMBARRASSING MYSELF that crippled me with anxiety. Experience showed me that when I was confident about what I was talking about; I had no trouble talking to whomever no matter the size of the audience. I just was not a BS-er; I could speak confidently only about things I KNEW about, and to know something implies experience. The same is true today—I feel way more comfortable speaking to audiences about my experience than anything else. In fact, I won't get up and talk to audiences when I can't speak from a place of genuine authenticity.

It's amazing what EXPERIENCE can do for you; just look at what it did for me. While teaching, experience taught me to be careful with what I say, and sometimes it's better to say nothing at all. Experience taught me to be a coach as well as a teacher. As Coach, my objective has always been to help my students, mentees, and clients recognize and tap into their own power. As Teacher, once I figured this piece out, my job has always been to optimally facilitate an environment where those with whom I work are meaningfully engaged and learning the subject matter while learning to learn. Experience taught me that I had something to share with my peers and fellow educators who did not have as much experience and to share it. Experience also taught me to listen and learn from those who had more experience than me. The list goes on.

And, aside from what experience taught me, experience also *prepared* and *equipped* me to join a small but mighty group of elite college educators whose primary purpose was to train and empower other college professors across and throughout the country in the art of student engagement, active learning, and student success. In this role, I'd frequently speak in front of large audiences comprised of college faculty, academic advisors, deans, provosts, college presidents, etcetera. And the topics I'd speak about were topics that I was genuinely confident in and passionate about due to my interest and experience. The practice role afforded me in speaking was invaluable.

Looking back, I credit that initial and clear intention for setting my speaking journey in motion. Pulling strings for my ultimate benefit, the Infinitely Intelligent Universe has always had a way of nurturing my growth by easing me into positions that would prepare and eventually ease me into yet larger positions to come. By being CLEAR, I didn't confuse the Universe with what strings to pull.

So, I would have to say that I got started in the speaking industry with a CLEAR INTENTION.

My Advice to Aspiring Professional Speakers

a.   If you think you have a fear of "public speaking," then learn to laugh in the face of that particular fear, which takes lots and lots of practice because that's not it. If you are anything like me, then your fear is not of speaking publicly; your fear is of embarrassing yourself (by appearing to "not know" what you are talking about), which is the result of a lack of confidence (stemming from a lack of knowledge and a lack of preparation). Time and committed interest will eventually endow you with all you need to become authentically confident.

b.   Start with a sincere and clear intention from where you are. Notice that I began in formal education and ascended the trajectory of that space over time. Now I speak from my authentic place on my terms, which involves how to prime your mind for optimum health, living a life of yoga beyond postures and poses, as well as The 12 Radical Intentions™ and how to live The R.I.C.H. Life™ (Radically Intent on Cultivating Happiness™).

c.   Find something wholesome that attracts your interest so much that you CAN'T NOT give it your attention. Become an expert in the subject by immersing yourself in the material of your interest. Learn it in whatever way your own curiosity guides you. Then organize your knowledge (create presentations, write books, and create classes) so you can know it better and get clearer. Live it, speak it, write it, publish it, teach it, and seize the day!

ABOUT DAMON

In 2015, Damon formulated an acronym for R.I.C.H., which stands for Radically Intent on Cultivating Happiness. He then went on to co-create and develop the *R.I.C.H. Life*™ philosophy and *The 12 Radicals Intentions*™ with his wife Kiala. In addition to that, Damon is the author of *Optimum Health Mindset (OHM): How to Think to Undo Fat, Maximize Your Vitality, and Never Get Sick Again*, as well as *YOGA, Truth, & The Real Fountain of Youth*. For at least the past 18 years, Damon has been on a quest to learn what's fundamentally necessary to heal physically and how to live the highest quality life possible, and yoga has been integral to his path. He was introduced to yoga for the first time just after the turn of the millennium, and from 2006 to 2007, he along with Kiala, attended and completed his first yoga teacher training, which consisted of 200 hours in Ashtanga Yoga/Vinyasa Flow at *Bliss Yoga* in Jacksonville, Florida. Five years later, from 2010 to 2012, he completed a 500-hour teacher training program in Viniyoga at the *Healing Yoga Foundation* in San Francisco, California. At the time of this publication, he's a student with Yoga Well Institute in an advanced, 1000-hour training and is on-track to becoming an internationally certified yoga therapist. Damon combines all he knows about yoga, healing, cultivating life conditions that lead to Happiness (with a capital H), and the spectrum of yoga tools beyond the mat into unique and powerful practices that help people transform in the greatest ways at the deepest levels.

LESSONS LEARNED FROM DAMON

What caught your attention? What are your takeaways?

16
Find the Topics That Really Make Your Heart Sing
By KIALA GIVEHAND, MFA, Ed.S
Happiness Catalyst | Empowerment Coach for Women

How I Got My Start

Like many things in my life, I didn't set out to become a professional speaker. It was something I stumbled into, found I was pretty good at it, and continued to hone and polish my skills. My first experience as a paid speaker happened in college when I formed a campus organization called Powerful Women's Coalition (PWC). As president and founder, I was offered several opportunities to speak and engage with young women and the leaders of groups dedicated to women. From Girl Scouts of America to school-based clubs like Future Business Leaders of America (FBLA), I was paid (albeit very little) to share my experience and journey to inspire and empower young women. That's when I realized I had a knack for speaking and sharing from the stage. It just came easily. And even though I considered myself, back then, to be an introvert, I was able to muster the courage to stand in front of a crowded room and speak, teach, or train people how to be the best version of themselves.

Little did I know that those small speaking opportunities would give me the foundation and confidence I needed to move on to larger stages with more audience members who had a greater desire to hear what I had to say. It was the steppingstones of those early speeches and talks that paved the way for me to become a professional educational trainer.

Once I started training teachers and administrators in education, I realized that I could do the same kind of speaking and on topics like creativity, self-empowerment, intuition, intentional living, and positive mindset. That's when I began actively seeking events where my speaking skills would serve me well. I spent seven years training faculty and administrators on various educational strategies and techniques, and those training sessions eventually helped me land regular contract work with a high-profile publishing company where I traveled the U.S. delivering presentations and workshops to help teachers feel more empowered and supported in the classroom.

To date, I've delivered more than 500 speeches, presentations, and workshops. Not all of them were paid, but each one taught me a little something about myself and those kinds of lessons are invaluable.

My Advice to Aspiring Professional Speakers

The most important piece of advice I can offer to aspiring professional speakers is to practice and prepare. Practice and preparation can come in many forms. For me, it always starts with a bit of visualizing. I see myself on the stage speaking or in a workshop setting, engaging with my audience. I hear myself giving the speech. Right down to snippets of the exact words I might say. I hear the laughter in just the right places, the silence when I say something moving, the scribble of pens on paper as they document the words that resonate with them, and of course the roaring applause at the end. I feel the excitement in my heart as I walk out on the stage. I engage all of my senses before I even get the offer to speak. This is how I manifest my dream gigs.

Of course, this is just the start. Practice and preparation also show up in the form of carefully selected topics that make me giddy. There are probably a thousand things we could each talk about, but finding just the right few will take you a long way. Find the three or four topics that really make your heart sing, then hone and polish those with consistency and confidence. These will become your signature talks and you MUST be enthusiastic about the ones you choose.

Once you've selected the right topics and visualized yourself speaking, the last part of practice and preparation is to actually say "YES" to offers to speak. When you're starting out, it may be prudent to say "yes" to one or two unpaid gigs so you can practice. Think of the free gigs as dress rehearsals for the paid opportunities. In the beginning, you need real stages with real audiences to help you gain confidence, find clarity in your topic, and build your speaking résumé. The more you practice, the more you progress.

ABOUT KIALA

Kiala Givehand is a published poet, bookbinder, teacher and workshop leader, fountain pen collector, and radical nomad. She believes in surrounding herself with ordinary humans who live extraordinary lives, gathering with people who allow her to laugh and love uncontrollably, and living a life intent on cultivating happiness. Kiala is a double Capricorn and an ambivert who grew up on the Gulf Coast of Florida where she learned to appreciate and respect hurricanes; humidity; and the transformational powers of the sun, the moon, and the ocean. She holds six academic degrees in various subjects from various universities, but the one she cherishes most is her Master of Fine

Arts in Creative Writing and Poetry from Mills College where she fell in love with book art.

In her day-to-day life, Kiala empowers women to live more fully and intentionally. She guides women who want to liberate their creativity, explore deep inner work, experience radical transformation, and create a life filled with passion and purpose. In her professional speaking life, Kiala has delivered more than 500 talks, speeches, presentations, and trainings to thousands of people all around the world. Her signature talks include "Passion & Purpose: The Introverts Guide to Engagement;" "Strategize & Thrive: 12 Ways to Live a Life Radically Intent on Cultivating Happiness;" and "Creative Empowerment: The Power of Intuition and Intention."

Kiala's writing has appeared in *Brush Magazine*, *Mabel Magazine*, *Calyx: A Journal of Literature by Women*, *Cave Canem Anthology XIII*, Eleven Eleven, Jacket 2, the Bella Vista Art Gallery, and in the Campanil. She is a SoulCollage® facilitator, a Cave Canem fellow, a Voices of Our Nations (VONA) alum, and a member of Delta Sigma Theta Sorority, Inc. Kiala obsessively studies astrology, sacred geometry, mandalas, and other ancient intuitive systems as a way to know herself more fully and compassionately. Through online courses and in-person retreats/workshops, she teaches women all over the world how to find what makes them happy and pursue it without regrets.

LESSONS LEARNED FROM KIALA

What caught your attention? What are your takeaways?

17
Always Take the High Road
By TRAVIS HARDIN
Inspirational Speaker | Mentor to Purpose-Seekers

How I Got My Start

I started the moment I truly understood what hopelessness was. I was in college and had seen far too many people give up on their hopes, dreams, and in a couple of instances, life. It is then when I said I wanted to "STAND" for those without a voice, and I began to speak out. More than 20 years later, the passion grows to provide a voice to those who would otherwise give up because of the assumption that no one cares. Many others and I truly care.

My Advice to Aspiring Professional Speakers

Always take the high road. Daily challenges and obstacles are going to come your way. Your management or mismanagement of these opportunity nuggets are vital to your growth. Some of my most memorable relationships and opportunities to add value by speaking have traced back to moments when I took the high road of life when I truly wanted to allow my frustrations to get the better side of me. Your ethics must revolve around giving yourself away.

ABOUT TRAVIS

With his purpose in mind, Travis continues to speak into the hearts and minds of listeners around the globe. As an inspirational speaker and leadership facilitator, Travis openly shares his heart about a world with instant addicts with a purposed, self-reflective transparency to which all audiences can relate.

LESSONS LEARNED FROM TRAVIS

What caught your attention? What are your takeaways?

18
What You Have to Say Matters
By CLINTON HARRIS
CEO | Influencer | Speaker | Entrepreneur

How I Got My Start
I initially started in the professional speaking business indirectly. I lived through a very tumultuous childhood. My childhood became my catalyst to want more positivity in my life, so I sought it out. I was always a positive force in my neighborhood, and many came to me for advice or motivation to brighten their outlook or plight—even in my early years.

As an adult, I found myself linking up with the likes of Brendon Burchard at one of his companies and became a part of his organization. I was a positive person that now had a positive organization propelling me forward. Although I felt supported, I still felt something was missing. I left the Brendon Burchard family on an epiphany as I'd decided it was time for me to be the person that I knew was hibernating inside.

I wrote a novel in 28 days, started my own coaching company, and started public speaking on a new level. Yes, I had spoken many times before for organizations, for military events, and for believing in one's self, but my speaking took on a newfound zeal that has since continued to grow to help any and everyone outperform his/her past and navigate towards positive change.

My Advice to Aspiring Professional Speakers
The one most important piece of advice I would impart upon those that aspire to be professional speakers is to understand that what you have to say matters and is profound. Many people that are in the

fledgling stages of this profession ask themselves, "Why would anyone want to hear what I have to say, and what do I have to say that's truly important?" The truth is your story and/or your perception and insight. We all have a story, but not all of us have the courage or desire to disseminate that story for the purpose of helping others on a grand scale. With that being said, if you are taking the time to read this book, and this passage, then you have the desire, now you simply need the tools and the belief that your words can have profound reverberations within another person's life. Believe in yourself and your purpose and follow-through until you reach your goal of speaking, then keep doing it. You will gain experience and more confidence as you progress along with the notoriety that comes along with it. Just do it: don't stop, and you will reach your goal.

ABOUT CLINTON

Clinton Harris is a personal development expert, life progression coach, entrepreneur, keynote motivational speaker, and #1 best-selling author. He has worked with many well-respected experts in his field. Working in organizational leadership, organizational leadership, educational institutions, with families and the military, he has served to help people all over the world for over a decade.

LESSONS LEARNED FROM CLINTON

What caught your attention? What are your takeaways?

19
Make Time and Room for Your Speaking Career to Grow
DR. MICAELA HERNDON
Chief Executive Officer, MHerndon Enterprises, LLC

How I Got My Start
There will never be a perfect season to start your career as a speaker so just start! I realized that I missed out on years of living my dream as a speaker because I was looking for a time to start. Then, one day, my mother reminded me of what I experienced in elementary school. This was the first time I had ever truly considered speaking.

When I was in the fourth grade, my class was discussing the intersection of religion and history. History has forever been one of my favorite subjects. I was engrossed in the lesson, and I held on to my teacher's every word. After the lecture, my teacher looked at the class and asked if anyone had anything to say. I raised my hand, thought carefully about my response, and I spoke. My teacher said, "Class, hold on one second." She left the classroom and went to get another teacher. I was asked to repeat what I said and both teachers were in shock. After all these years, I can't remember what I said, but I can remember one thing. My teacher said, "Micaela, you have something to share with the world, and when you're an adult, don't be afraid to speak."

Speaking is something that came naturally to me, but I don't believe a person has to be naturally gifted to speak. Anyone can speak, but the art of speaking is about having something to share with an audience in a way that influences change. In order to create this influence with an audience and secure speaking engagements, it is imperative to develop three things: your purpose as a speaker, your target audience, and a speaker framework.

My Advice to Aspiring Professional Speakers

As a speaker you want to have a "why." This is going to allow you identify your signature talks and will give you the ability to create an identity as a speaker. You may be tempted to do all the speaking engagements you are offered in the beginning of your career, but do not take them all unless they fit your branding. It is important to identify engagements that will grow your branding and allow you to gain more attention from targeted clients.

Figuring out your target audience as a speaker is not only important but it is imperative. Your audience is reflective of the people who will be most impacted by your experience. For example, if you are doing diversity and inclusion training for all ages, then the curriculum needs to scaffold throughout the age groups in order to increase its effectiveness. You would not want to give a group of elementary students the same training that would be given to a Fortune 500 company. Your audience reflects your trained voice, and choosing an audience will grow your niche.

You should never "just go speak." Speakers plan, customize, and practice the content of their speaking engagements repeatedly. Even if you are giving the same training or keynote for a similar agency, it should be specific to that client even with the core of the information remaining the same. When you plan, you are developing a framework for your style of speaking. For example, I don't start with a salutation but a well thought-out introduction to grab the audience's attention early. Research different speakers, develop your own voice, and practice.

I didn't get into the business of speaking overnight. It took a couple of years to start to garner the national attention I desired. My speaking career excelled after I casted a vision, set goals, and took time to invest in my craft. I enrolled in a speaker boot camp that showed me how to refine my skills as a speaker. I created short-term and long-term goals. Mostly important, I believed in me!

Some of you who are reading this may be working full-time and feel limited on how much you can commit to your speaking career. Remember, there is always time to invest in your dreams. I began by using my lunch breaks to go to coffee shops for 45 minutes each day and focus solely on my speaking business. When I started to speak, I made a video to let my family, friends, and professional colleagues know that I was looking for opportunities. Within 48 hours, I had over 15,000 video views and started receiving national speaking opportunities. This was because I made time and room for my speaking career to grow.

ABOUT DR. MICAELA

Growing up in Dallas, Texas with a single mother and an incarcerated father, Dr. Micaela Herndon developed a keen sense of awareness, a highly developed mind for critical thinking, and mastered the power of perseverance. With storytelling as her core skill, she has built a strong reputation for motivating audiences in unforgettable ways. As an experienced national speaker and educational professional, Dr. Micaela has been featured on CBS, Fox, and ABC News. She has worked across multiple disciplines and age groups as a keynote speaker and consultant to develop leaders and to help audiences find their purpose and create a new sense of personal identity.

Dr. Micaela uses her personal and professional experiences to create a fresh perspective with her audiences that encompasses visionary inspiration and that plants seeds of change.

LESSONS LEARNED FROM DR. MICAELA
What caught your attention? What are your takeaways?

20

Find What Makes You Unique and Lean into It
By ALANA M. HILL
Speaker | Author | Consultant

How I Got My Start

I started speaking as a project manager for a technology company. As part of my role, I gave presentations to garner support for new projects, and I provided training worldwide to implement the changes. It started as technical projects, and I began to lead other business change initiatives. They all had one thing in common: they needed me to speak to a room, and I loved every minute of it. That was the start of phase ONE of my speaking career—corporate presentations and training. Phase two started after I left the company for which I worked and when I started a consulting business. I trained my clients, presented, and gained even more expertise. During the first 10 years in business, I worked virtually, providing online training, virtual coaching, and meeting face-to-face only on an occasional basis. This was giving me the flexibility I needed to raise my four boys and to serve in my community. I knew I'd rejoin the friendly skies when my kids were older.

When my oldest son was diagnosed with cancer, my motivation for speaking shifted to uplifting people and helping them build faith and resilience. I soon realized how many people in my professional world needed that message as the economy and industries struggled to remain viable. I then started speaking at conferences in my field of project management, emphasizing the need to lead change and develop resilience. That became my message. My experience as a project manager gave me insight into how to create a framework that people could follow in their personal and professional growth.

My Advice to Aspiring Professional Speakers

Start where you are already known and respected. Leverage that expertise and learn what you are worth early—don't spend a lot of time "giving yourself away." If you are speaking on a subject matter on which you are an expert, the mechanics of the speaking business may be new, but your skills are not. Don't treat yourself like a rookie, and you won't be treated like one.

I've heard it said in different ways, but find what makes you unique and lean into it. Don't run from your story! Find ways to integrate all your parts into this wonderfully, unique message with an amazingly distinct delivery. Do YOU!

Once you decide that you want to become a professional speaker, join Toastmasters to practice your craft and to work through your message, and join National Speakers Association (NSA) to learn how to build a speaking business. Like anything new, create a plan and work that plan. Set goals for yourself and your business and measure them.

ABOUT ALANA

Change comes naturally to Alana. An outgoing soul who moved around a lot as a child, she learned to adapt to her environments. Having lost her mother to violence when she was only 17, Alana learned early how to develop resilience. Alana took that strength to work with her when she graduated from college with an engineering degree. Adapting to the demands of the oilfield, she rose to the ranks of program manager and led change initiatives for a global oilfield services company. Alana is a certified project management professional (PMP) and leverages her expertise in project and change management to help individuals and organizations excel— even in the face of adversity.

Alana's highly acclaimed third book, *What's Your Catalyst? The Power of Managed Change: How Purpose and Passion Can Drive Strategic Life Change*, gives readers a dose of inspiration and a serving of actionable strategies to help them lead change in their personal and professional lives. She guides readers to go beyond her story, in her first two books, AND into their own. She leads them to explore their passions, talents, and paths to becoming more effective leaders at work and at home.

LESSONS LEARNED FROM ALANA

What caught your attention? What are your takeaways?

SECTION 2 ACTION PLAN

Based on what you learned from the contributors in this section, what action will you take?

SECTION 3

21

Know Your Audience and Create the Best Content for It
By WENDY KAAKI, PhD
Professor | Educational Consultant | Mentor/Coach

How I Got My Start

I got started as a professional speaker when I was teaching at the college level. My students and director told me that I should start speaking publicly and reach out to others besides those who were in the classroom. Then my supervisors would ask me to create presentations on topics of their choice and present them for fun. I was persuaded by a small audience because I was able to deliver speeches impromptu without rehearsing when I attended a junior college. One professor told me that one day I would have a huge room of people staring at me and waiting for me to speak and that they would not get bored. I never paid attention to that comment until today as I remember him telling me that this is a gift.

My Advice to Aspiring Professional Speakers

My one piece of advice to aspiring professional speakers is to know your audience. It is very important to know to whom you are speaking so you can create the best content for them; this information not only helps you create content but also helps you discuss what they want to hear and understand as you have already uncovered that with which they struggle and that about which they want to hear. When you present ideas that are not of interest or concern, then you will not get as much attention, and your listeners may not use what you present to their benefit. If you create scenarios and activities specific to the group, then they can better relate to and are more familiar with the content, and can use what you share with them.

ABOUT DR. WENDY

Wendy Kaaki, PhD is an educational leader, keynote speaker, educational consultant, and coach/mentor. She has served for over 25 years in post-secondary institutions across the globe, holding titles such as associate professor, academic dean, campus director, associate provost, and campus leader. She enjoys international cooking, coffee, and music. She is involved in community volunteering and loves to attend museums. Dr. Kaaki is always involved in creative ways to improve the lives of others. Dr. Kaaki has been involved in career and technical education, college and university educational programs, curriculum development, accreditation, student and faculty satisfaction as well as institutional effectiveness.

LESSONS LEARNED FROM DR. WENDY

What caught your attention? What are your takeaways?

22
Be Strategically Audacious
By CRYSTAL KADAKIA
Two-Time TEDx Speaker | Culture Change Expert | Best-Selling Author

How I Got My Start

I was working a full-time job while exploring business ideas on the side—not to just get free from a normal nine-to-five but because I truly wanted to help people. I felt like the corporate structure wasn't allowing me to make an impact. I achieved a certificate in coaching and tried that as a side gig but found out that it wouldn't be sustainable full-time. Along the way, I kept noticing that I had a different point of view emerging on one of the hottest changes going on in the workplace: generations. I decided to share my thoughts at some chapter meetings for the Association for Talent Development, the largest professional association related to training professionals. After two talks, I decided to apply to speak at a nearby TEDx event. This was a crucial moment—and a very audacious move on my part. I dove into public speaking—I dove deep. I learned very quickly that my voice mattered. At the end of a very successful TEDx talk, I had companies approaching me to speak for a fee. I realized that not only was this sustainable, but it had the power to impact people positively—to truly create change.

I wanted speaking to lead to consulting. I kept on setting audacious targets—all very specific to reaching the people who most needed to hear my message regardless of how different I was or how much confidence was needed to stand in front of them. My target audience has been executives, and I found them since the day I started at age 25. I no longer speak only on generational change, but

I speak and consult on a wide variety of workplace culture changes that are essential to people thriving in a digital world.

My Advice to Aspiring Professional Speakers

Be strategically audacious. If there is any one thing I want everyone to know, it is those three words. Life is short, and we often don't take the obvious, shortest path to what we want. We say, "Oh, I'm not ready to do that" or "It's too risky to invest in that," or we spend too much time recycling thoughts and overthinking things. Ask a few people how to get to what you want. Google it. Then, craft your next steps. Make your goals and your path audacious but not unintelligent. Don't risk money you don't have. But if you have money, be willing to invest it in what data shows will make a difference. Some of us invest a lot of little amounts of money in a lot of things rather than picking the top-of-the-line resource and taking the leap. All those little moves can often move you backward or keep you stuck rather than move you forward. Don't let your mind get in the way of your audaciousness. Believe that your voice and your story matter, and make your decisions from that point forward.

ABOUT CRYSTAL

Crystal is a two-time TEDx speaker, international keynoter, and best-selling author known for transforming the toughest workplace challenges into exciting possibilities for our digital world. As an organization development consultant, she brings organizations into the digital age, leveling up people strategies in areas such as career development, learning culture, inclusion, leadership development, and employee engagement. Past clients include General Mills, Southern Company, Monster.com, Wells Fargo, and other organizations. She also brings deep training expertise as the co-creator of the Owens-Kadakia Learning Cluster Design model that upskills the training industry to design modern learning, which is supported by the Association for Talent Development (ATD).

Through her best-selling book, *The Millennial Myth: Transforming Misunderstanding into Workplace Breakthroughs* (Berrett-Koehler, 2017), and keynotes, Crystal has changed the story around generation gap for thousands over the past decade. Her most recent book, *Designing for Modern Learning: Beyond ADDIE and SAM* (ATD, 2020), calls for a transformation of the training industry, empowering relevancy in the digital age. Her current project is a deep study of self-leadership actions that help create connection, escape burnout, and overcome other challenges unique to the digital age.

Crystal is honored to be a Power 30 Under 30, CLO Learning in Practice, and ATD One to Watch award recipient. Her academic background includes a bachelor's degree in chemical engineering and a master's in organization development. Originally from Austin, Texas, she is now based in Atlanta, Georgia with her husband, Jeremy, where they love immersing in nature's way of life and cultural experiences.

LESSONS LEARNED FROM CRYSTAL

What caught your attention? What are your takeaways?

23
Level-Up a Few More Notches
By GANES KESARI
Co-founder and Head of Analytics, Gramener, Inc.

How I Got My Start

I've found writing[1] and speaking[2] to be the best ways to share knowledge and give back to the community. I co-founded my data science startup, Gramener, in 2010. Soon after, I started speaking to demystify data insights, and I integrate storytelling with data. Over time, I've made it my mission to make data science simple and accessible for everyone. I regularly speak at events to help executives apply data science and build their team to realize business value from data.

I truly believe that you master a topic only if you are able to explain it to a lay audience, in simple language. A key milestone in 2019 was my TEDx[3] talk where I explained artificial intelligence (AI) in simple English to a general audience. I used storytelling to show how AI is saving the planet and our endangered species.

My Advice to Aspiring Professional Speakers

I would strongly recommend aspiring speakers rehearse and record their gigs. While you may not have to script it, a few rehearsals can make a world of difference. It helps you gather the thoughts, practice your delivery, and smooth the flow. When you're in front of the audience, you can then focus and connect with them instead of processing your content. You can level-up a few more notches by recording the video of your rehearsals and the final gig. It took me a while to get over the awkwardness of watching myself on video. However, it was transformative in ironing out things and giving myself subtle feedback that others may have missed.

ABOUT GANES

Ganes Kesari is the co-founder and head of analytics at **Gramener**[4]. He advises executives of large corporations as well as the senior leadership of non-governmental organizations (NGOs) and governments. He is an expert on the application of data science and helps companies build effective teams and adopt a data culture. Ganes is an international speaker, corporate trainer, and a passionate writer. He is on a mission to simplify data science and help everyone understand its true potential. Check out his latest pursuits at https://gkesari.com

[1]https://gkesari.com/write/
[2]https://gkesari.com/speak/
[3]https://www.youtube.com/watch?v=hqM3nYwcSso
[4]https://gramener.com/

LESSONS LEARNED FROM GANES

What caught your attention? What are your takeaways?

24
Return to the Roots of What Works
By ROBERT "BOB" KIENZLE
Senior Consultant, Knowmium

How I Got My Start

The first formal speech I remember was in my high school public speaking course. The class was fun, and I did well; this feeling continued through to my bachelor's degree courses at the University of Arkansas. At the time, I never considered public speaking (and the many professions that require it) to be my career path. A couple years later, I was working for a non-profit organization in Denver, Colorado and was assigned to perform periodic presentations and briefings. The topics were often left up to me, and this is when I first realized I had a passion for presenting. I loved the freedom to choose my subject, share my opinions, and educate others for the greater good.

My role as a presenter quickly changed the next year when I was accepted into a master's communication program back at the University of Arkansas. I was offered to teach the intro-level communication and public speaking courses. Now, I was being paid to publicly speak as an instructor and was publicly speaking about public speaking. I was challenged to learn new theories and methods of presentation (along with other communication theories and skills) and deliver them professionally to regular groups of students, a.k.a. paying customers of the university. I learned to balance nervousness with confidence and juggle the demands of my instructor role with the demands of my full-time master's degree. I simultaneously took research, consulting, and intern roles at for-profit and non-profit organizations. These roles helped me diversify my experiences in business communication.

My success in academia and my desire to see the world led me to South Korea. I quickly made my way back into the university world, teaching at Sungkyunwan University, Korea's oldest and one of their best. I instructed Korean students, foreign students, and university professors in presentation, writing, business communication, cross-cultural communication, and lecturing/teaching skills. During my time, I got involved in Toastmasters International first to network with other English-speaking professionals and later to refine my own speaking skills on stage.

I once again found my passion for choosing and delivering my own topics: my hobbies, my travels, my political and social views, and my fondness of using visuals and props to keep audiences smiling. I dove into other non-profit organizations and education groups and kept delivering formal presentations at regional conferences.

Through networking and exposure on-stage, I made my way back into paid business speaking and consulting. Year after year, I was onboarded into communication training programs for companies around Asia. I was also developing my own workshops. I was being paid to fly from country to country to train finance employees, managers, and executives. Once again, I found the balance between my role as an academic instructor and corporate facilitator and speaker. When I became tired of balancing two industries, I moved completely into corporate training and speaking engagements with a bit of non-profit volunteering and graduate school instructing on the side. I still give fun speeches in Toastmasters International and other social groups when I have free time.

My Advice to Aspiring Professional Speakers

Find the balance between business best practices and your personal uniqueness. Be ready to share what works for most businesspeople and what might work best for individuals and your audiences. By showing your own style on stage or in the board room, you'll be engaging and memorable. You will also help your audiences and learners explore their own styles as they grow their own communication skills. Return to the roots of what works: To what do humans pay attention? How do humans perceive and process information? Then create something you've never done and that they've never seen before. They've seen TED Talks. They know what a good presentation looks like. Now show them something fresh. Make them think, make them talk, and make them interact. They'll likely call you again and give your number to their contacts. You'll have quite a bit of fun, too, even if you don't get to sleep much the night before.

ABOUT ROBERT

Robert is the senior consultant at Knowmium in Hong Kong and facilitates persuasive communication programs and coaching for global firms throughout Asia and beyond. His programs focus on keynotes, presentations, storytelling, influence, negotiation, writing, and many accredited assessment programs. Robert is a Distinguished Toastmaster in Toastmasters International and was a World Championship of Public Speaking semi-finalist in 2014 and 2015. Originally from Fayetteville, Arkansas, he has 15 years of business and education training experience in the markets of Asia, North America, Europe, and Africa.

LESSONS LEARNED FROM ROBERT

What caught your attention? What are your takeaways?

25
Your Message is Someone Else's Medicine
By ARTESIAN D. KIRKSEY
Author | Transformational Speaker | Mental Skills Coach

How I Got My Start

I became a professional speaker by accident. Yes, you read that correctly—by accident! I was always shy when it came to speaking in public or having to present in the classroom as a student. It was not until I became a college professor who had to lecture daily in front of my students that I became more comfortable and confident in my ability to speak. I would find unique ways to keep my students engaged by telling stories that related to the topics we discussed while sprinkling in some inspiration and even some transformational thoughts. Students would constantly tell me how motivated they were after my lecture.

I did not just want to inspire people; I wanted to help them marry their potential to the right mentality.

It was not long before I started hosting the new student and faculty orientations. This eventually led to me being asked to be the keynote speaker for several college graduations and receiving invitations to come share my message at a multitude of events. It was almost as if each time I spoke at an engagement, I would receive an invitation to come speak at another.

I learned how to use my environment and platform as a higher education professional to practice my speaking craft daily until I felt comfortable enough to actually start charging for my services.

My Advice to Aspiring Professional Speakers

Just get started! Always remember your message is someone else's medicine. If you know you have a message and you believe in it, share it with anyone willing to listen. You need a M.A.P.

Mentor: Once I became serious about speaking and making it a business, I decided to start researching potential mentors who were seasoned professionals and who had successfully accomplished the goal I was trying to achieve. I did my research and finally identified someone who had been in the industry for about 15 years, getting results and outcomes at a very high level. This is the person I contacted and asked to be my mentor. This will save you so much time and energy that you'd otherwise waste by trying to "figure it out." Doing this will help set you up for success. Studying under the tutelage of my mentor helped me learn so much more—both about the art of speaking and the business aspect of this industry. Mentors are priceless; invest in one.

Action: Once you've identified your mentor(s), the real work begins. You must start taking action and get in your speaking "reps." This is critical because in order to master your craft, you need to speak at any and everywhere you can in order to cultivate your message and identify your target audience. Even if you initially speak for free, I challenge you not to view this as a waste of time. This actually provides you with an opportunity to practice and improve your craft. Aside from that, people in the audience will not know nor will they care that you were not compensated for your services. There may be someone in the crowd that wants to offer you a paid opportunity once they hear your message. The goal is to expose as many people as possible to your message. One of the things I did was contact all friends, family, and former co-workers and let them know I was pursuing speaking. I let them know if they needed a speaker for any event, then I was their man.

Process: This is the most important step. You must understand the process associated with becoming a professional speaker. You don't have to love it; you don't even have to like it. However, you must respect it. Everyone's journey will be different, but one thing's for sure: you will receive many "no's" before you get one "yes." It's okay; that's all a part of the process. Even the most successful speakers in the industry have experienced this. You need a strong mindset, and most importantly, you need to practice what you preach. I learned long ago, people will follow your example well before they follow your advice. The profits you seek are a byproduct of respecting the process.

ABOUT ARTESIAN

Artesian Kirksey is a United State Marine Corps veteran who served honorably in Afghanistan during Operation Enduring Iraqi Freedom. While serving on active duty, Artesian took advantage of the advice and mentorship offered by the senior Marines in his unit. It was at this time that he made the conscious decision to further develop his own leadership style. He attributes much of his success and overall character development to the Marine Corps. In an effort to give back, he decided to become a transformational speaker and a mental skills coach.

Artesian earned an MBA in addition to having a master's degree in higher education with an emphasis in adult teaching and learning.

After completing his military enlistment, he began working in the field of higher education. Artesian has over 15 years of experience and has had the extreme pleasure of working with students from all walks of life throughout the various phases of their college experience. He has been fortunate enough to have had the opportunity to serve as a college professor, dean of faculty, and dean of student affairs.

In addition to his extensive background in higher education, he is also the founder and CEO of Artwork, LLC, which offers curriculum in the areas of mindset, personal development, and professional development. He recently published his first book titled *The Art of Transformation*.

His current mission is to transform lives, one mindset at a time.

LESSONS LEARNED FROM ARTESIAN

What caught your attention? What are your takeaways?

26
Take Inspired Action
By VERED KOGAN
Executive Coach | Speaker

How I Got My Start

I got started in the speaking business in the same way that many of us created good things in our life—by *setting a clear and meaningful intention*, *focusing my attention* on that vision, and then *trusting my intuition* regarding what actions to take to make that vision come to life.

It all started when I read the book, *Think and Grow Rich* by Napoleon Hill and learned about the power of intention and focus. I set an intention to become a professional speaker, and I took time every morning to mentally rehearse that new future by visualizing myself on stages, making a positive impact, earning a great income, and enjoying the experience. The more I got into the FEELING of being a professional speaker (even though I had not yet been paid to give even one talk!), the more my brain started giving me new ideas about how I can make that vision a reality.

For example, I got the idea to join the National Speakers Association (NSA), enter into a Toastmasters International speech contest, attend certain events, connect with certain individuals, and so on. I chose to take actions every day that moved me closer to my vision. It was hard work—I often had to step way out of my comfort zone—but I did it because it felt aligned, and I believed in myself. What I didn't know it at the time is that my daily habit of imagining and focusing on what I wanted was priming my brain and body for the changes that were about to take place.

Within a few weeks, I was invited to become a speaker with Vistage Worldwide, Inc., an organization that facilitates peer-advisory groups for CEOs and key executives around the world. I now speak with groups all over the country on topics that are deeply meaningful to me, and I've had the opportunity to connect with many extraordinary individuals and to speak at their organizations.

My Advice to Aspiring Professional Speakers

I believe that every person is capable and deserving of creating the life he/she desires. Most people believe that working very hard will allow them to create what they want. I believe that taking action is absolutely important, however, it is often not enough. Many speakers work very hard but do not achieve the goals they have set for themselves. The key is to take *inspired* action. How can you do that? You can do that by doing the "inner" work to get yourself ready for the future that you desire.

When you practice imagining or visualizing your ideal future and you focus your attention on FEELING the way you will feel when you achieve that goal, you are programming your mind to BELIEVE that this new reality is possible for you. This allows your unconscious mind to access new ideas and intuitive thoughts regarding the best actions to take to achieve what you want in the quickest and most enjoyable way. In other words, you will shift from simply taking action to following your intuition and taking inspired actions that feel aligned with your vision for your ideal future. You feel comfortable letting go of things that are not directly aligned, and you immerse yourself even more in those activities that intuitively feel right. It is all about FOCUS. When you consistently make decisions that feel good and are aligned with your vision as a speaker, it is just a matter of time until the right opportunities will show up in your life!

ABOUT VERED

Vered Kogan is an author, speaker, and transformational coach focused on helping corporate leaders and entrepreneurs harness the power of human performance and potential. Throughout her life, she has been on a quest to inspire and lift people to higher levels of personal and professional fulfillment. She is a leading behavioral and mindset expert with a unique ability for helping people release the mental and emotional obstacles that prevent them from achieving their full potential.

Vered began her career as a civil engineer and went on to earn an MBA specializing in strategic management. She then joined PricewaterhouseCoopers as a management consultant, helping business executives prepare their organizations for change. Vered holds numerous professional coaching certifications, is a trainer of neuro-linguistic programming, board-certified hypnotherapist, HeartMath Institute trainer, Rapid Transformational Therapy practitioner, and certified yoga nidra instructor. She has helped hundreds of people adapt more effectively to change and create the lives they desire.

Vered is a member of the National Speakers Association and has won numerous speaking awards including being voted a "Top 10" Vistage speaker in 2018.

LESSONS LEARNED FROM VERED

What caught your attention? What are your takeaways?

27

Do Not Let All of the "No's" Discourage You

By TORI KRUSE

Founder and President of Highlights 'n Heels® | Empowerment Speaker | Coach

How I Got My Start

My journey to becoming a professional speaker has been quite unusual! Growing up, I loved playing sports and watching college football, so I thought I would eventually become a sports reporter, standing on the sidelines next to Erin Andrews. I graduated college from the University of Iowa with a bachelor's in entrepreneurial management. After college, I moved to St. Louis, Missouri for an outside sales position selling commercial flooring. For about three years, I worked for this company, and although it was a great job and I worked with great people, it wasn't something about which I was passionate. At this point in time I had already competed for Miss Iowa Teen USA 2010, Miss Iowa USA 2013, and Miss Missouri USA three years in a row. My last time competing at Miss Missouri USA 2017, I placed first runner-up, and I decided to quit my sales position and move to Los Angeles. I kept my home in Missouri and Airbnb hopped for seven months while I modeled and pursued my ultimate career goal at the time—sports reporting. Once my seven months were up in Los Angeles, I went back to my home in Missouri to compete at Miss Missouri USA 2018. This was my sixth time competing, and I finally won! This is the time I realized that I wanted a career with a microphone in my hand, but instead of reporting a football game, I wanted to share my own story about overcoming challenges to help inspire others. My journey to becoming Miss Missouri USA was not an overnight success. It was a total of eight years of personal growth and learning multiple mindset and confidence techniques to overcome every single "no" I received. Throughout my reign, I spoke throughout the state of Missouri, and after crowning my successor a year later, I founded my public speaking and coaching company, Highlights 'n Heels®. Now I speak and coach women and young adults on embracing uncertainty, developing confidence, and overcoming fear. I'm so passionate about sharing my story and life obstacles to help inspire others on their personal life journey!

My Advice to Aspiring Professional Speakers

Gosh, it's so hard to just pick once piece of advice, but I would say the most important thing to remember is not to let all of the "no's" discourage you. I was told "no" more times than "yes" before I was crowned Miss Missouri USA. If I had given up every year I didn't get crowned, then I never would have walked on the Miss USA stage or impacted all of the lives I did with the crown and sash, which was one of the biggest rewards of all. Oftentimes, we start to doubt ourselves if we're not getting booked, but it's the consistent work you put in behind the scenes that no one sees that will end up paying off the most. If it's in your heart and you're deeply passionate about what you speak on, it will shine through you and people will book you when the timing is right. Be patient, and NEVER GIVE UP!

ABOUT TORI

Tori Kruse is an empowerment speaker and coach for women and young adults looking to overcome challenges and increase confidence. Tori was crowned Miss Missouri USA 2018 and advanced to compete at Miss USA 2018. She's received training from top experts in personal development such as Tony Robbins, Dean Graziosi, Rachel Hollis, and Jen Sincero. Tori works closely with her clients to develop positive mindset techniques that dramatically improve self-esteem and enable them to conquer life's challenges.

She developed a seven-week coaching program that is tailored to each client's specific needs, goals, skills, and opportunities. Tori blends her academic training and professional development insights, bringing her clients and audiences a wealth of experience and understanding of their personal goals and objectives. She has been featured on ABC, CBS, FOX, NBC, *E! News*, INSIDER, *OK!* and *Cosmopolitan Magazine*. Tori holds a bachelor's degree in entrepreneurial management from the University of Iowa. She was the co-founder and president of the Iowa Retail Association and studied international marketing in Florence, Italy. She is also an active volunteer and regularly serves with the Special Olympics.

LESSONS LEARNED FROM TORI

What caught your attention? What are your takeaways?

28
Don't Compromise Who You Are or What You Speak About
By CHERY KUBA
Gerontologist | Author | National Speaker

How I Got My Start

There are probably dozens of speakers like me. I started speaking before I ever thought about speaking. My area of expertise was dealing with adult children of aging parents and what adult children should expect as they become family caregivers.

At a time when I was working as a regional marketing director for a long-term care housing company, I was listening to a speaker the company had brought in to motivate our team about sales and marketing. As the program went on, I found myself drifting away from her content and focusing on her platform skills, speaking capabilities, and humor. The thought that stayed in my mind was "I want to do what she's doing."

I contacted the speaker, Maureen O'Brien, and we met at her home so that I could learn more about the actual business of speaking. Shortly after, a friend showed me a flyer about a local Association for Applied Therapeutic Humor meeting. At that meeting, one of their members introduced herself to me and asked what I would like to gain from the meeting. It turned out that this woman was Deb Gauldin. president of the Illinois chapter of the National Speakers Association (NSA). She invited me to the next NSA meeting. I attended and joined the organization. NSA and its members have been the foundation of my speaking and learning as an author, national speaker, and eldercare expert. I went on to become the president of the Illinois chapter and its Humanitarian of the Year.

My speaking engagements, in the beginning, were to small audiences, and the fees became higher as my experience in speaking and marketing grew. My first audiences included church groups, seminars, rotary clubs, and libraries. I didn't burst onto the scene commanding mega-money deals. But publishing my first book, with a different hook about eldercare and caregiving, *Navigating the Journey of Aging Parents*, became my entry into larger audiences and more lucrative contracts.

My journey as a new speaker was a good learning experience with many hits and a few misses. I continue to learn, tweak, and adjust. I am so grateful to have had guidance from the masters and support from both family and friends who believed in me. I love what I do, and it is always exciting to step up to the mic.

My Advice to Aspiring Professional Speakers
Speak everywhere to any size audience.

Size doesn't matter—for the perfect audience.

For the more than 18 years that I have been a professional speaker, my largest audience to date is one that also gave me the most media exposure. And I was speaking for free. My audience was primarily women since this was a Smart Women/Smart Money conference put on by the state treasurer of Illinois and former state senator, the late Judy Baar Topinka.

Although there was no speaking fee for this event, the benefits were many:

- The media exposure was phenomenal because the conference happened on the day Judy Baar Topinka announced that she was running for governor of Illinois. She entered the grand ballroom of the Hyatt Regency Hotel in downtown Chicago in a blaze of glory with the media trailing behind. I was positioned right next to her on the stage, so every photograph of Judy included me.

- Each presenter was offered, at no cost, a table for 10 guests to attend the luncheon—an opportunity to invite current and potential clients as well as people to whom I wanted to offer a "thank you" of sorts.
- As noted earlier, this was my largest audience ever.
- I was also humbled and honored to have some heavy hitter, seasoned business professionals sharing the stage with me that day.

Speaking to a handful of people.

My target audience for 18 years was adult children of aging parents and family caregivers. (I am identifying my *former* audience because when this book comes out, I will have transitioned into a new topic for a different audience. Stay tuned.)

My "handful of people" audiences were both successful and lucrative. A business friend of mine invited me to give my talk to a group of her friends who were all family caregivers. The venue was a beautiful sunroom in her home. My talk and the discussion that followed were a success, and each participant bought my book. The hostess, Maureen, said to me after the event, "This is you. You should travel the country with a love seat stapled to your [bottom] and talk about caring for parents and your book." She held several more "living room chat" events for me, and all were abundantly successful with the return on investment in so many ways.

There is also the opportunity to present to small groups for big money. Mine have been audiences of eight to twelve business leaders at a luncheon for my **full speaking fee**.

World-renowned professional speaker Larry Winget often tells about the start of his career, speaking to not-so-interested people in church basements—many of whom were sleeping during his talk.

Stay in your lane.

Don't compromise who you are or what you speak about to get the job. If you speak about eldercare, don't throw your hat in the ring for a presentation on leadership in property management just because you have an open place on your calendar. Instead, contact meeting planners and other speakers who have similar topics, and offer your availability if they have a cancellation at the last minute.

ABOUT CHERYL

Award-winning author, nationally recognized speaker, and adventure seeker Cheryl Kuba is speaking from the road while living the dream by traversing the US in the family motorhome.

Cheryl works with organizations that help their clients turn dreams into reality. She guides clients through building a roadmap so they can live it, dream It, and do it! Her passion is fueled by thunder, tenacity, and grit, and for Cheryl, perseverance means make it happen!

Seeking adventure and a new lifestyle isn't without its detours as Cheryl learned when one phone call delayed the family's journey for 18 months. As a gerontologist and eldercare expert for the last 30 years, she knows that when a family member needs help, you answer the call.

It took a leap of faith to reverse her master's thesis about information available to family caregivers to diving deep into what Care Receivers and the dependent elderly really want. The result is an award-winning book, *Navigating the Journey of Aging Parents*, published for a worldwide audience. Two other books followed, *21 Life Skills for the Desperate Family Caregiver* and *Faith Lessons*.

A sought-after expert in her field, Cheryl has been featured in *Men's Health*, *The Chicago Tribune*, *Minneapolis Home News*, *ADWEEK*, *Advertising Age*, *Back Stage*, *Screen*, and *Suburban Life's Daily Herald*. In broadcast media, Cheryl has appeared on the Christian Broadcast Network and has shared her expertise through interviews with many media outlets. She also hosted a radio program, Care Radio, on Chicago's WIND-AM Radio.

Her work in spiritual leadership comes from a foundation as a minister of care (commissioned), a Stephen Minister, and continuing course training in clinical pastoral care. She has spent several summers officiating Cowboy Church in Grand Lake, Colorado.

Cheryl believes that one should spend a portion of every day making someone's life better through love, friendship, and compassion.

To contact Cheryl A. Kuba, MA-Gerontologist
www.3happycampers.com
cheryl.kuba@hotmail.com
773 327 9331

LESSONS LEARNED FROM CHERYL

What caught your attention? What are your takeaways?

29
Create a Strong Speaker Network
By SANDRA LONG
TEDx Speaker | Author of *LinkedIn for Personal Branding*

How I Got My Start

I am an accidental speaker and enjoying my second career. In my early years, I did some company-related speaking as a corporate executive, but it was usually in front of my team, customers, or colleagues. I did okay, but at that time, my speaking was secondary to my sales or leadership mission.

In my second career, I leverage my unique subject matter expertise. I am an independent LinkedIn consultant, speaker, instructor, and author. I began with writing and teaching. In the beginning, I spoke at chamber and SCORE events, which were uncompensated. My most enjoyable and profitable speaking opportunities now are at corporate events or for company teams. I also enjoy speaking at conferences and universities.

My speaking is greatly enhanced by my book because many of the companies or universities that hire me will purchase books for the attendees. Writing a book also helps me to get found. Readers sometimes reach out for me to speak at their organizations.

Now, most of my speaking opportunities come from referrals or people contacting me after discovering me on Amazon, LinkedIn, YouTube, or Google. I also maintain a strong network of speaker friends who help me, and I co-lead a professional speaker group in Connecticut. Being connected makes a huge difference!

My Advice to Aspiring Professional Speakers

Speak whenever you can. I am a big believer in practice, practice, practice. I diligently practice for every single speech. Even speeches that I have done over and over still require practice sessions.

I have used some of my volunteer or pro-bono talks as a chance to practice while also giving back to a non-profit organization. Everyone wins.

When I practice alone, I always time myself to make sure I am on target to keep within my allotted time on the agenda. I am not memorizing the talk, but I want to be very comfortable with the opening, closing, and the overall flow. My talks are tailored to the audience, so the practice is critical.

My other advice is to create a strong speaker network. In addition to many speaker friends, I have been actively involved with three different speaker groups. The best speakers help each other along the way!

ABOUT SANDRA

Sandra Long is an independent LinkedIn consultant, author, and speaker. Her specialties include branding, networking, social selling, and social recruiting. She is the author of the Amazon best-selling book, *LinkedIn for Personal Branding: The Ultimate Guide*. Sandra is also a 2019 TEDx speaker. Her talk is entitled "LinkedIn Community: A Super Power Hiding in Plain Sight" and is now available for viewing on YouTube. Sandra is the president of Post Road Consulting, LLC in Westport, Connecticut. The company's clients include sales teams, corporate C-Level executives, HR teams, universities, and recruiters.

LESSONS LEARNED FROM SANDRA
What caught your attention? What are your takeaways?

30
Allow Yourself Space to Fail, Learn, and Grow … Fall in Love With the Process
By CLAUDIA S. LOVATO
Speaker | Educator | Professional Problem Solver

How I Got My Start

I began public speaking at a very young age. As the youngest of a large family of seven, the only way to be heard was through effective communication.

My dad once said, "Kid, you have a big mouth, and you never stop talking. If you can find a way to get paid for talking, you'll be in pretty good shape."

He was being funny but had no idea how that statement would shape my future. He was the most powerful speaker I have ever met, and his level of influence on me rivaled that of the likes of the Tony Robbinses of the world. He was a leader in the labor industry, a teamster that often participated and lead pickets/movements for change, and was also a mentor to many young men.

When I came across people who worked for him, their eyes would light up, and then they would go into how much they admired my dad—how much he helped them strive to be their very best.

This was the type of person I wanted to be. Before I started hearing how my dad had influenced people, he was just my dad. How he spoke to me was just how he spoke.

Looking back, he made every word count. He had such a way of stringing thoughts together. The funny part was that he was not a talker. He just happened to put a lot of thought into what he wanted to say, and his words were impactful.

At a young age, I got into dentistry and fell in love with the profession. Not long into it, I saw so many areas of frustration and inefficiencies. I started writing down solutions. I began speaking up during staff meetings and unofficially became the spokesperson for my co-workers who would say, "You should speak for us. You have a way with words."

It didn't take long before I transitioned out of the dental clinic into speaking and consulting. But it all started with writing and getting my papers into the right hands. This was before Facebook and social media, so that was very difficult to do and was a very slow process.

I started speaking at study clubs and doing in-office team building workshops, and I eventually got invited to speak at large conferences.

If I could credit any specific efforts or tasks that helped me get into speaking, it would be building relationships and serving others.

Once I got involved in social media networking, I did not immediately promote myself and my business. I connected. I listened for needs. I observed others. If I could fill a need, I offered. If I knew someone else who could fill the need, then I made the connection.

I eventually created my business pages and began promoting them. I invited my entire network over to follow my business pages. Some went. Most did not. This was perplexing. I asked a social media expert what I could do to remedy this "problem." She told me they would not go. They obviously preferred following my personal page and having a more personal connection to me.

What I had done was organically connect with like-minded people in my industry and build authentic relationships.

Many of those friends were influencers, podcasters, and board members for their state associations. If they had a need I could fill, I offered, but oftentimes, they came to me.

This was not work. This was just a path I chose while learning about social media. It also comes naturally to me to serve.

I am currently an educator, speaker, consultant, and the owner and founder of an organization that helps speakers and consultants advance their careers.

My Advice to Aspiring Professional Speakers
Be patient. It doesn't happen overnight. It takes hard work, persistence, and investing in mastering your craft.

Don't quit your day job! The biggest mistake I see aspiring speakers make is getting into speaking for the wrong reasons. Some are working in toxic environments and just want a way out. The speaker lifestyle appears to be easier, glamorous, and financially rewarding.

The truth is speaking does not offer a steady and dependable stream of income right away. Even once you get established, you will be in a sales position, trying to get yourself booked. That is a full-time job in itself.

Being a great speaker takes a lot of creative energy. It is difficult to be creative when you are stressed about making your mortgage and car payment.

Create a plan to carve out time to dedicate to writing, attending speaker training programs, and networking.

Learn to pivot and be adaptable. Be open to change.

Be kind to yourself, and allow yourself space to fail, learn, and grow.

Fall in love with the process—even the ugly parts and the growing pains.

Pick a message that you are passionate about. If there is no passion in the story you're telling, then you're telling the wrong story.

Get out there, and do some good in the world!

Best wishes to you on your career journey!

ABOUT CLAUDIA

Claudia began her career in dentistry as a dental assistant in 1995. Her first experience of "saving someone's teeth" was a pivotal moment in her career. It was then, she knew she had found what she was looking for—a challenging and rewarding career centered around serving and helping others.

Claudia's personality is that of a restless spirit who cannot settle for the status quo.

In 2005, she began to focus on solutions to common problems that plague dental practices.

Since then, she has been a writer of continuing education (CE) curriculum, an educator, speaker, dental podcast host, mentor, consultant, and friend to all in the dental industry. She is currently the program director at Arizona College in Mesa, Arizona.

As founder of the Morado Dental Academy and Morado Allied Speakers and Consultants (Morado ASC), Claudia has scouted and assembled resources for professionals to engage in educational workshops, practice management support, event facilitation, seminar presentations, and speaking and consulting training.

Claudia is known for her heart for service and her ability to inspire all people to work at higher levels of efficiency and cohesiveness. Her passion for all things dental and collaboration with some of the brightest people in dentistry are what led Claudia to create the Morado Dental Academy and Morado ASC, a soft landing place for professionals where you will find encouragement, support, learning programs, and systems to help you reach and exceed your goals.

Claudia believes that all things are possible when done with a furious passion and the drive to put in the work!

LESSONS LEARNED FROM CLAUDIA

What caught your attention? What are your takeaways?

SECTION 3 ACTION PLAN

Based on what you learned from the contributors in this section, what action will you take?

SECTION 4

31
Be Real, Risk Vulnerability, and Be More Human
By RACHAEL MANN
Author | Public Speaker

How I Got My Start

Several years ago, I was tasked with training a group of high school students on how to speak in public for classroom presentations and state and national conferences. As I determined how to go about teaching presentation literacy to these students, I thought back to how I learned how to speak in public. I realized that the closest I got to being taught public speaking was in a speech writing class in college, which was more along the lines of reading to an audience and looking up from my notes at key moments. I also thought back to my junior year in college when I almost dropped out of the teacher prep program after my college professor announced to the class how many times I had said "ummm" during a lesson I was delivering. Mortified, I called my mother to inform her that I was dropping out of the program. My mother said something along the lines of "Suck it up, buttercup." I got back to work on finishing my degree.

I wanted to ensure that this group of student leaders had a more meaningful experience and that they learned how to truly use their words to connect with an audience. I decided to turn to TED Talks to learn how the greatest TED speakers prepared for their 18 minutes of fame and impact on the red circle, and I began using the resources that I discovered to train this group of high school students to become leaders as Educator Rising State Officers. As I saw their abilities transform from timid and scattered speeches to powerful presences with impactful narratives, I thought of how the brain science behind what captures an audience's attention might have transformed my classroom lessons as a teacher. I pondered how this skill set could have enabled me to have a more confident approach to sharing ideas in board meetings, leading professional development workshops, or speaking to the community. I developed a presentation to deliver at conferences with 10 principles to apply in order to teach or present in an effective way that were loosely based on the TED Commandments that are given to speakers who are invited to the main TED stage. The requests for this presentation, both as a workshop and as a keynote address, became greater, and eventually, I formed an LLC and launched my new business titled #TeachlikeTED.

My work has since grown, and the #TeachlikeTED concept morphed into one- to two-day workshops called "Turning Ideas Worth Spreading Into Talks and Presentations," and my love of disruptive technologies and space exploration have paved the way for other keynote addresses on projected changes in the workforce and how to ensure that, as a society, we are equipped for what is yet to come.

My Advice to Aspiring Professional Speakers
An important aspect missing from the narrative above is my dread of speaking in public. Yes, you read that right. I am a public speaker with HUGE anxiety about getting on a stage! One of the most important pieces of advice that I would offer to aspiring professional speakers is to get started now. Say "yes" to every opportunity to share your ideas and your voice. Unless there is a strong "no," say "yes." Don't wait until you feel comfortable speaking in front of crowds. Don't wait until you are poised, polished, and perfect. You will soon find that most speakers never feel that they have "arrived." Most work their entire careers to perfect the art. The comfort level, the poise, and the perfection will develop to some degree; however,

your audience also wants someone who is relatable and real. Some of my presentations that have been the best received and were given outstanding evaluations are ones that I felt were sloppy while I delivered them. I could feel my voice quiver and my knees shake, but the message truly came from the heart. Your audience wants to see and feel your humanity. Be real and risk vulnerability. Be more human.

If your purpose and message are too important not to share, you can't NOT get on the stage or behind that microphone even if your knees are shaking. Develop routines to help you stay focused and that ensure you remember why the audience needs to hear what you are saying. Remind yourself that it's not about you; it's about how this message will impact the individuals in front of you. Channel your nervous energy into excitement. If your message hits home for at least one person, your talk was worth every drop of nervous energy. If it hits home for more than one person, then you have to keep going. You have found your calling and your destiny.

ABOUT RACHAEL

Rachael Mann is passionate about all things related to education, technology, and science. She is an "edufuturist" who believes in the importance of shaping the educational philosophies and spaces of today by looking toward the innovations of tomorrow. Rachael is a frequent keynote speaker at STEM-related events, and she speaks and writes about disruptive technology, education, and careers. She is the author of the children's book, *The Spaces You Will Go* and coauthor of *The Martians in Your Classroom*, an educational title about integrating STEM into the classroom utilizing space-related initiatives.

Rachael holds a Master of Arts in Educational Leadership and has 14 years of classroom teaching experience in a range of subjects, including child development, science, technology, and culinary courses. Ms. Mann's experience includes her work as the Network to Transform Teaching state director, the professional learning director of STEM, and the Arizona State Director for Educators Rising. She is a founding member of the Council on the Future of Education and serves on a number of national boards that are dedicated to ensuring that kids are future ready.

She lives with her husband in Phoenix, Arizona and enjoys tennis, hiking, good eats, and traveling.

From professional growth to motivational talks to workshops, Rachael loves to inspire audiences to think bigger and dream beyond. Connect with Rachael on social media @RachaelEdu to learn more about her work.

LESSONS LEARNED FROM RACHAEL

What caught your attention? What are your takeaways?

32
Set Your Audience on Fire!
By BRIDGETT McGOWEN
International Professional Speaker | Author | Publisher

How I Got My Start

For me, it all started with my elementary school report cards. It never failed; I excelled academically, but at the conclusion of a grading period, teachers would consistently write in the comments section "Talks too much." As an adult, I thought "Hey. Why not put that to good use?!"

Seriously, though, my speaking career began with me watching others present, then making presentations myself at professional conferences, which did *not* pay, then being placed in a position where I *had* to start charging for my speaking.

In 2002, I began teaching for the Lone Star College System and the Texas A&M University System. However, I had received no formal education in how to teach. I was hired because I had the necessary credentials, and I was provided access to resources that were designed to provide teaching best practices. I immersed myself in learning as much as I could about the twenty-first century commuter college student and the residential university student, post-secondary teaching methodologies, and overall best practices when teaching adults, which led me to attending conferences, workshops, symposia—anything I could find to get an understanding of how best to reach my students and, once I became a lead instructor, how to support my colleagues. About 90% of the time, I would take what I learned back to my campus and recreate workshops for my colleagues.

While attending those presentations, though, I would observe the speakers and say to myself, "I can do THAT!" As such, I started submitting my own proposals, and what do you know?! Conference organizers were accepting my conference session proposals left and right! I even had a following of sorts where conference-goers would come up to me and say, "I don't know what you are presenting. I came just because I saw your name on the program, and I knew it would be good!" My goal in all my presentations was— and still is—to set people on fire. I wanted to give valuable information and simultaneously ignite a flame that made people want to jump up, run out, and take on the world with their new knowledge.

Eventually, my husband and I relocated from Texas to Arizona, and in 2009, I started presenting faculty development and professional development workshops full-time for an educational technology (edtech) company with a team of the smartest and most creative professionals I've ever met. I absolutely loved it! For more than seven years, I traveled the country, designing and presenting workshops and webinars to faculty and administrators at colleges and universities all over. Those workshops and webinars focused on the very concepts I has worked so hard to understand during my first years as a faculty member—how to reach the twenty-first century college student, post-secondary teaching methodologies, and overall best practices when teaching adults. When asked what I did for a living, I would proudly reply with the answer I'd adopted from one of my managers, "I teach professors how to teach."

One of my teammates at the time was Damon Givehand, and in 2013, his wife Kiala Givehand, saw me present at a conference in New Orleans where Damon and I were presenting along with our teammates. She immediately told me I needed to start my own business. I thought to myself, "Yeh, right!" The truth of the matter was I was perfectly happy with the work I was doing at the time and had no intentions whatsoever of or any interest in starting a business. We shared a joke at the time about her surreptitiously purchasing my domain name then, when I came to my senses and decided to open the doors to my company, she would offer the URL to me for a ridiculously obscene amount! (She didn't do that, but what vision she has!)

The edtech company went through many changes, and the next thing you know, my entire team of colleagues was disbanded; we were all laid off. In short, I knew what I loved to do, and that was to design and deliver high-energy presentations. As a result, I created my own company in April 2016; and the rest is … well … you know!

There was a steep learning curve, though. Yes, I knew how to design presentations, own the room, and wow a crowd, but running a business was a whole other situation.

Just days after the layoff, I had a conversation with Damon and Kiala, and within a few weeks, I purchased my first domains, www.bridgettmcgowenhawkins.com and www.bmctalks.com; however, I sat and looked at them for months. I'm not kidding. I didn't know where to start or what in the world to do with them! I had not performed any website design work since around 2000 or so, and of course, anything I may have remembered from then was completely obsolete.

Finally, in June and with the help of Kiala, I figured out how to build a site. In July 2016, I purchased and established my LLC so others could see and regard me as a serious business.

In August 2016, I landed my first serious speaking gig. The requestor found me on thumbtack.com, reached out, and we had a phone conversation so I could learn about what the company wanted in a speaker. Because of my limited experience—not as a speaker but as a speaker who spoke on the topic the company wanted—I offered to provide a 30-minute demo of the presentation. About a week later, I facilitated, via Zoom, the demo for three or four team members at the company, and within five minutes of the demo, the lead person who had initially contacted me stopped me and said, "I don't need to see any more. You're hired!" His colleagues unanimously echoed his sentiment.

I continued to consistently market myself as a professional speaker, submitting proposals to speak at conferences where I knew my ideal client would be in the audience and, as often as possible, where I knew big names will be on the agenda.

In November of 2017, I decided to use my maiden name, Bridgett McGowen, as my professional name because let's face it; Bridgett McGowen-Hawkins is just too long and too complicated! (When I approached my husband, Aaron Hawkins, with the idea of using my maiden name as my professional name, he said, "Fine by me—as long as the name on the checks is correct." He's a riot!) In June 2018, I purchased a third URL, www.bridgettmcgowen.com, using it as my primary speaker site while using the first site, www.bmtalks.com, for my academy services. (It took me only five days to design the second site thanks, in large part, to the help of a speaker bootcamp.)

I have since launched BMcTALKS Academy, an online academy that offers self-paced modules and mini-courses on presentation skills plus modules on how to launch and grow a professional speaking business, as well as my independent publishing company, BMcTALKS Press.

The number one obstacle I faced in the beginning process of starting my professional speaking career was knowing where to start and wanting to have everything perfectly in place, but perfection is not necessary. It's not. Believe that!

My Advice to Aspiring Professional Speakers

Do not wait for the perfect moment or the perfect situation. Get out there and present. It doesn't matter the venue or the size of the crowd. Get out there, demonstrate yourself as an expert in your field, and brand and hold yourself out as a professional speaker. Seek out conferences, conventions, symposia, forums, workshops, and expos with target audiences that can benefit from your message, and apply to speak so people can start to recognize your expertise and that fact you speak on it. Do not wait for the perfect moment or for everything to be perfect. Take one step, then another, and simply keep moving forward with intention and purpose.

And when you do speak, be fierce. Be bold. Be outstanding. Be completely unforgettable. With everything you do, do it full-out and in an extraordinary fashion. In short, as an audio/visual professional told me after hearing me speak and as I was preparing to give an encore performance at a conference in November 2019 in Raleigh, North Carolina, "light 'em up!"

Set your audience on fire!

Perform in a manner that makes you unforgettable for all the right reasons. You want people to walk away from your presentations, and years from now, they may not remember your name or what you wore. They may not even remember the content of your talk, but because your delivery was so infectious, so flaming-hot until they remember the passion, energy, and excitement that accompanied your message. They remembered how you made them feel. In short, show up and show out!

I once had someone ask me what that means—to show up and show out. Here goes: Be mentally and physically present when you make presentations—don't just go through the emotions or assume you have a captive audience just because you have the mic—and give everyone a reason to listen to you. Give them a show that's electric, one that has the room completely on fire because you have two options. You can be common and ordinary, or you can be completely extraordinary.

Own the microphone. Light 'em up. Set them on fire! You've got this!

ABOUT BRIDGETT

One thing that's a guarantee is if you attend a presentation facilitated by Bridgett McGowen, then you will not soon forget it! Bridgett is a Forbes contributor, a publisher, an author, and an award-winning international professional speaker who has designed and delivered hundreds of high-impact webinars, keynote addresses, and workshops to thousands of professionals all around the globe, and there's absolutely no doubt that she LOVES what she does! When Bridgett is on the microphone, there is never a dull moment because audience members talk. They move. They write. They laugh! Oh … and they learn!

Bridgett is a native Texan; the founder and owner of BMcTALKS, LLC and the BMcTALKS Academy; the CEO and owner of BMcTALKS Press; and the creator of *Own the Microphone.*

LESSONS LEARNED FROM BRIDGETT

What caught your attention? What are your takeaways?

33
Create Your Power Story
By Dr. Will Moreland
America's #1 Leadership Life Trainer

How I Got My Start

That's a great question. "How did I get started in the speaking business?" I had been speaking for almost 15 years, but I wasn't in the speaking business. Individuals and organizations had asked me to share my story for different events over the years, and as a pastor, I spoke six to seven times a week—three times on Sunday and three to four times during the week—but I never considered myself a professional speaker. People thought my story of a young kid coming out of Compton, California; a former drug dealer; and gang banger was inspiring, and I enjoyed sharing it. I never imagined in a thousand years that I would actually get paid to tell my story, and I never thought I would travel to over 40 countries to share my story.

In 2010, I transitioned back to the United States from living in Germany for 15 years. While in Germany, I started a consulting company that did very well. Life was good; I was pastoring three churches and running my consulting company. In 2009, I decided it was time for a change. I felt there was more for me to do. I felt a nudge telling me I had become comfortable with success, and I wasn't hungry any longer.

Like any well-intentioned entrepreneur, I packed up my family and moved to Arizona. With my dreams in hand, my faith on high, and a wife who was five months pregnant, we moved to a state we never lived in before—a place where I had no contacts, no business connections, and just the nudge that I should be doing something different.

I had it all planned out. We would live off our savings for about a year as we transitioned back to the United States. My wife would have the baby, I would have the opportunity to invest some time with the family before I jumped back into the mix, and everything would be amazing. A simple enough plan, right? Wrong! Very wrong. The first roadblock we encountered was trying to get insurance for my wife and soon-to-be-born son. We were unexpectedly told that my wife had a pre-existing condition that prevented her from being insured. As I nervously read the letter, we called the insurer and asked, "What condition did my wife have?" They replied, "She is pregnant." Well, yes, we know that; that's why we need insurance. To make a long story short, we were not able to get insurance, so footing the bills for pre-natal care and the birth of my son was coming out of pocket.

This put a small dent in our savings plan and my plan in general. This meant I was going to have to get back in the swing of things a little sooner than had I planned. But no big deal. I had built a successful company in Germany. How hard could it be to do it in Arizona? With my positive attitude and can-do behavior, I set out to conquer new territory. The only problem was Arizona, like most of the United States, was just recovering from the recession of 2008, so things were slow. The only problem with that—my bills were coming in fast.

After about eight or nine stressful months. I was frustrated, feeling defeated, second guessing myself, and ready to give up. And I would have if I didn't have a family that was depending on me. I had uprooted my family from a pretty comfortable lifestyle with promises of a bigger and even more exciting life.

With money running low and my faith almost on empty, I called a friend to go out to lunch to vent my frustrations. During our conversation, he mentioned something that would change my life forever and usher me into the speaking business.

I like to call myself "**The Accidental Speaker**." It seems funny typing those words because I have been blessed to travel all over and impact lives in 40 different countries on five different continents. I have spoken for Fortune 500 Companies, I have been invited to the White House to Speak, and 1,500 presentations later, I now have the pleasure of training other speakers to build thriving speaker businesses through our Genius Speakers Academy. Not bad for a person who didn't even know the speaking industry existed.

Now back to the conversation that changed my life and got me into the speaking business. While talking to my buddy, he said, "Man, you should start speaking." When I think back to the initial look I gave him when he said that—as the saying goes, "If looks could kill." Here I am pouring my heart and frustrating out, and he is talking about I should start speaking.

You see, when he said those words, all I could think about was all the many times people had asked me to speak before. At the end, I would get a gift card, a plaque, or some "token of appreciation," which I never had a problem with because I enjoyed sharing my story. But at this point in my life, I didn't need any "tokens of appreciation;" I needed money. I guess my friend could hear the disgust in my voice and see the look on my face. He said, "You know, I just received a check for $3,500 to speak at a company today." I quickly replied and said, "WHAT! How much?" He replied "$3,500 for a 45-minute talk."

He had my attention now. He went on to explain that he had left his corporate job and was a full-time professional speaker. In hindsight, this sounds silly, but I didn't know that this profession existed. The funny thing is I had listened to Les Brown, Tony Robbins, Zig Ziglar, Jim Rohm, and many other motivational speakers, but it didn't click that there was a whole industry of speakers out in the world.

My friend mentioned that there was going to be a speakers conference and that I should attend. At this point, I had nothing to lose and agreed to go to the conference with him. When we got to California, I was blown away. There were over 1,500 speakers at this conference. My mind was blown away.

It was during this conference that "**The Accidental Speaker**" was born, and I entered the speaking business—a choice that has transformed my life and my business and has afforded me a life beyond my dreams.

My Advice to Aspiring Professional Speakers

Early in my speaking career I had the privilege and pleasure of meeting a GIANT in the speaking Industry. I remember our encounter like it was yesterday because it almost didn't happen. On that day I received a call from my business partner, he said, "Hey, man. Les Brown will be in town tonight. Let's go see him." It had already been a long day, and we would have to drive about an hour or so to see Les. My body was telling me "no," but I knew this was a great opportunity to meet a legend.

I was standing in the lobby of the hotel when none other than the great legend himself walks in. I didn't want to bother him as I knew he had to speak. But in true Les Brown fashion, he noticed me and walked over and greeted me. As fate would have it, I got the opportunity to invest about 40 minutes with Les right there in the lobby. Before I walked away, I said, "Mr. Brown, if you could give me one piece of advice to hold on to as I build my speaking business, what would that be?"

Without hesitation, he replied, "**DEVELOP YOUR STORY**."

And this is the same advice I would offer to anyone wanting to have longevity as a professional speaker. Your life is filled with lessons, successes, failures, wins, and losses. Dig deep into these experiences and capture what I call your "**Power Story**." Les told me that day that his "**Power Story**" had earned him over $65 million. My ability to find, harness, and deliver my "**Power Story**" has been worth millions to me.

Here is a short blueprint on how you can create your "**Power Story**."

Step 1: Break down your life in five-year increments.

Step 2: Give each time frame a name. For example, from age 20 to 24, I call this "Exploring."

Step 3: After you give each time frame a name, look for a theme or pattern in your life. For me, the theme is "CHOICES."

Step 4: Now start to build a story around that theme. For example, "When I look at my life, I can see the better my choices, the better my life."

Step 5: Pull out the best stories in your life that highlight your theme.

Follow these five steps, and you will be well on your way to creating your "**Power Story**."

Speaking has been a dream come true for me, and I hope the same will be true for you as you continue to build a thriving speaker business and IMPACT lives around the world. m

ABOUT DR. WILL

Dr. Will Moreland is a military veteran turned serial entrepreneur, best-selling author, and business consultant. For the last 20 years, Dr. Will has traveled the globe to IMPACT * INSPIRE * INFLUENCE audiences, organizations, and individuals in over 40 countries on five different continents. An awarded business leader, Dr. Will has been named a Top Speaker, named a Top Speaker, Business Leader of the Year, and most recently was named an Ambassador of Civility. As founder of Will Moreland International, LLC, he is a consultant to Fortune 500 Companies, CEOs, professional athletes, and government officials.

Dr. Will is married to Dr. Kristie, and they have two children, Karah and Champ. The family makes their home in Phoenix, Arizona and St. Maarten.

LESSONS LEARNED FROM DR. WILL

What caught your attention? What are your takeaways?

34
Every Opportunity is Not YOUR Opportunity
By ANNETTE J. MORRIS, MA
Certified Life Coach/Business and Mental Health Coach | Author | Speaker | EntreprenHER

How I Got My Start

I started in the speaking business about 10 years ago as a result of conversing with someone about my life's story of overcoming poverty, being the product of a single-parent home, and other life struggles to successfully becoming a first-generation college graduate. I initially was called to speak in schools to audiences of high school students and in different churches and shelters to single mothers. I later started creating my own platform that allowed me to do more speaking to this same population when I realized my story was a story that gave hope to individuals who felt as though their life stories (that were similar to mine) were death sentences and success just wasn't in the cards for them. When I would speak to people, after I spoke, I realized I needed to share my story more to help individuals gain hope and fight for the life of their dreams— that the past life is not an indicator of a future life. This is what has caused me to keep pushing in this arena, being a hope pusher and dealer.

My Advice to Aspiring Professional Speakers

Every opportunity is not YOUR opportunity. As an aspiring speaker, it can be so tempting to jump on every opportunity presented to you in an effort to be more visible and to help with accelerating your speaking career. However, it's very important that you identify your niche, speaking topics, and target audience up front to avoid accelerating in the wrong lane. Please understand that the speaking arena doesn't lack opportunity and that your story will be most fitting for your target population ... God didn't design you or your story for EVERYBODY. Also don't resist investing in yourself. Connect with a mentor who can help you with homing in on your skills and guiding you to methods of securing speaking engagements. A mentor can assist you with avoiding the pitfalls and getting to your destination far more quickly. An investment in a mentor is an investment in your goals and your next level. I wish you much success on your journey to many stages!!!

ABOUT ANNETTE

Annette J. Morris, M.A. is a professional mental health counselor, certified life coach, motivational speaker, published author, entrepreneur, and business consultant. Her favorite quote is the philosophy by which she lives: "You will get all you want in life if you help enough people get what they want" by the late Zig Ziglar. Her professional career is focused solely on helping others to either accomplish their goals as entrepreneurs or in life as a whole. Although Annette has accomplished a lot in life, she had very humble beginnings. She was reared for 23 years in a local housing project by a single mother and had to overcome many obstacles on this journey called life. However, all that she's endured in her past has helped to form the Annette of the present. Annette is a first-generation college graduate and has earned a Bachelor of Arts in Psychology from Southern University of New Orleans and a master of arts degree from Xavier University of Louisiana. She's also the first full-time entrepreneur of her family and is the owner/lead consultant of Goal Getter, LLC. Annette has also published three books *Conquering the EneME, Live Free: Creating the Streams to Live*

Your Dreams, Everyday's a New Day: Daily Positive Affirmations for Positive Daily Living, and *Streams Reloaded: The Entrepreneur's Guide to Multiple Streams of Income.* She also co-authored a project entitled "I Want to Quit My Job: 8 Entrepreneurial Tips for Massive Results While Employed" and spearheaded a co-authorship project entitled *Favor in Failure: How Failure is the Key to Success.* Of all that she's accomplished in life, she's most excited about being saved and a child of the most high God.

LESSONS LEARNED FROM ANNETTE
What caught your attention? What are your takeaways?

35
Invest in Your Growth
By SIMONE E. MORRIS

CEO | Award-Winning Diversity and Inclusion Leader | Consultant | Speaker

How I Got My Start

My career has had many twists and turns. I started out as a trainer, then a developer and then a project manager in information systems. Early on, I realized I wasn't 100% comfortable when called to the front of the room. After an occasion where I trampled my words, I realized I needed help and joined a local Toastmasters organization. Somehow I made it through those first 10 speeches and found myself raising my hand to volunteer for leadership roles and to speak at the district conference. I really lucked out with some solid mentoring from Jeremey Donovan for my first conference speech. My proposal was selected, my delivery was well received, and a newfound confidence emerged.

It wasn't long before I found myself consistently up in front of the room combatting my fears. And, surprisingly, I was enjoying myself. I was able to begin showing up more confidently in the workplace. Even more so, my confidence about allowing my voice to be heard increased.

My speaking career took on a whole new life when I embraced my role as an employee resource group leader back in my corporate days. I volunteered to support the diversity and inclusion agenda by leading an African Heritage Employees group. What I found with the role was that there was going to be ample opportunities to share my viewpoint. And as such, the need to lead and be in the front of the room was ever present internally and externally to the organization. I found my voice and then began seeking out these opportunities.

One of those early opportunities was at the Working Mother Network & Affinity Leadership Congress (NALC) Conference. I spoke about executive sponsorship, and it was very well received; so I volunteered again the next year. This time, I was a moderator. It didn't feel all that great, and I knew I had to keep working on building my speaking muscles. I didn't give up, and I volunteered again for a third year. You know what they say; the third time is the charm. Having the success in the Employee Resource Group (ERG) space gave me confidence to continue my speaking path.

As I exited corporate America, I explored various avenues to consider as a business. It was clear to me that speaking was one of the things I thoroughly enjoyed, and so it became a core part of my business. I continue to seek speaking opportunities. I am fulfilled by sharing my core messages of career ownership and inclusive leadership with my audiences.

Growing as a speaker requires continual learning. The transition from Toastmasters to National Speakers Association (NSA) cemented my commitment to moving forward with a professional path for speaking. The NSA has been a helpful organization for the next chapter in my speaking journey. The alliance has allowed me to gain lots of knowledge around the business of speaking.

For the coming years, I can see that speaking will continue to be front and center for my career.

My Advice to Aspiring Professional Speakers

Join Toastmasters to build your speaking capabilities. Do not just join. Join and give it your all. I used to hide from Table Topics®[1]. I had somehow made it through the program without volunteering for this ad hoc speaking. It would take me a long time to see my avoidance of Table Topics® was doing myself a great disservice. Volunteer to speak and lead. It will build your communication skills.

Get clear on your speaking message. You need to know your title, speech summary, and the key objectives with which the audience will walk away. Spend some time on this. Create a couple speeches and test them out on your Toastmasters community.

Volunteer to speak everywhere. Tell people you're speaking and ask for the opportunity to speak. Create marketing collateral for your speaking business—a one pager, a website, and a video showcasing you speaking. Ensure the video is of professional quality and that it is recent.

Join NSA. Take advantage of the online groups for growth. Find a speaker friend with whom you can take this speaking journey. Take advantage of mastermind groups on social media. Black NSA and Power Women of NSA both have mastermind groups.

Invest in your continued growth as a speaker.

[1]Table Topics® is a Toastmasters tradition designed to help members hone their abilities to speak while thinking on their feet. During Table Topics® at a Toastmasters meeting, members must quickly organize their thoughts to succinctly and clearly respond to an impromptu question or topic.

ABOUT SIMONE

Simone E. Morris is CEO of Simone Morris Enterprises, LLC, a certified minority and women-owned business enterprise. She is an award-winning diversity and inclusion leader and a consultant and speaker committed to workplace and training women and emerging leaders to take true leadership positions in all aspects of their lives.

Ms. Morris has a background that includes over two decades in corporate America, spanning information technology, commercial strategy, and human resources. She holds an MBA from the University of Connecticut. Her technology background has served her well, embedding within her a strong project management acumen that allows her to educate and create transformational results for her clients. She teaches diversity and inclusion, conscious inclusion, and project management.

Ms. Morris shares her message across various platforms to include *Forbes, Medium, Thrive Global, Glassdoor, Leadercast, SmartRecruiters, Social Hire, Diversity Best Practices, Profiles in Diversity Journal,* and *BambooHR.* She is also the author of *52 Tips for Owning Your Career: Practical Advice for Career Success, The Power of Owning Your Career: Winning Strategies, Tools and Tips for Creating Your Desired Career,* and *Achievement Unlocked: Strategies to Set Goals and Manifest Them.*

She resides in Connecticut with her family.

LESSONS LEARNED FROM SIMONE

What caught your attention? What are your takeaways?

36
Learn From the Best
By MONICA NEUBAUER
Speaker | Podcaster | REALTOR®

How I Got My Start

When I started my career in real estate, I knew that speaking would be part of my future. I needed to learn how to do it before I could speak about it, though. Learn about real estate? Yes, learn the business so I could talk about the business. But what I also needed to learn was how to speak. I am a natural performer, so actually speaking in front of people was the easy part. But failing in front of people was not something I wanted to do at all! I wanted to be an excellent speaker. While I was enjoying learning and doing the real estate business, I was also learning how to be a speaker. There is much to learn about being a business owner and having a speaking business, but what is there to know about the skill of being a speaker? What skills are required? Being boring was not an option. I am an enthusiastic person and wanted to be an enthusiastic speaker. Being overenthusiastic is a thing, too. I want to walk in the balance of entertainment and education—to present something fun and valuable.

I started learning how to focus my words and messages through Toastmasters. I recommend Toastmasters to anyone who wants to be a speaker. I learned to structure a message with a beginning and an end, to recognize and minimize my filler words "um," "so," and "like." I received encouragement and direction in a supportive and serious environment with like-minded people in other industries. And after being introduced to other topics necessary to excel, I began to participate in other environments where I could learn, network, and practice my speaking skills. I attended speaker training events where I learned about managing the PowerPoint process, building it and running it while speaking. I studied humor and found ways I could incorporate humor into my speaking in ways that were and are comfortable for me. Skilled trainers taught me how to relate to and manage the audience with respect and control. I got a coach who helped me narrow my message and focus my ideas.

The best speakers are flawless in the execution of these skills. They are learned skills, even for those with talent.

My Advice to Aspiring Professional Speakers

I would suggest every aspiring speaker join Toastmasters immediately. Local chapters are in every city and most of them are open to newcomers. While improving your skills there, find a conference or training event where you can listen to great speakers and learn how to improve your technique in front of an audience. There are frequent train-the-trainer events in associations and companies designed to train future speakers and trainers. This is a great place to learn locally. There are also conferences and mastermind groups to help aspiring speakers as well. As you start networking and asking around, these organizations can be found by the seeking speaker. If your state has a local National Speakers Association (NSA) chapter, join it, and learn from the best. My state NSA chapter was an excellent place for me to be challenged and supported while learning and networking. Keep educating yourself while you are growing your business. When you focus on learning new skills in the area where you want to go, alongside your current job or work, you will be prepared for new opportunities when they arise, and you will be confident enough to move into that new situation. Always be learning and growing to help you be prepared in the current environment of change.

ABOUT MONICA

Monica Neubauer has been an entrepreneur since she graduated from college. She and her husband have lived on and visited four continents and many island states. They settled back into Middle Tennessee where she grew up and was part of Nashville as it went from sleepy city to Hipster Headquarters! Monica is the founder and owner of ClassicWhiteShirts.com. She has sold real estate since 2002 in the Franklin and Nashville markets. She travels nationally as a speaker to help people grow their businesses and hosts the Center for Realtor Development Podcast for National Association of Realtors (NAR). Monica is a former REALTOR of the Year. She loves helping people improve their businesses and lives life funtentionally.

www.MonicaNeubauer.com
www.ClassicWhiteShirts.com

LESSONS LEARNED FROM MONICA

What caught your attention? What are your takeaways?

37
Be Yourself
By JULIE NIESEN
Marketing Manager, Cisco Systems | Freelance Food Writer |
Marketer | Speaker

How I Got My Start
I started speaking on panels, usually about social media, food, or marketing. I can't recall what was the first panel I was on, but when I'm asked to speak, people tell me that my personality and thoughtfulness are why they pick me—not just my expertise. I started to get solo speaking opportunities after I honed my craft doing customer presentations during my days in academic publishing and training salespeople on social media. My speaking style is irreverent (but not insulting); informative; and, I hope, approachable.

My Advice to Aspiring Professional Speakers
Be yourself. Don't binge watch one person's TED Talk and try to be that person. Watch a lot of speakers. Read a lot. Figure out what your voice is and be true to it. Then, people both know what to expect, and you establish a brand for yourself. And have fun. No one wants to see a stodgy speaker. Figure out how *you* keep people interested.

ABOUT JULIE

Julie Niesen is an award-winning food writer, marketer, and speaker based in Cincinnati, Ohio. When Cincinnati had only newspaper and magazine writers, Julie saw an opening and took it, building *wine me, dine me* into an award-winning food blog. Currently, she works for Cisco Systems in thought leadership marketing as well as consulting, speaking, and writing for the local NPR speaking, and writing for the local NPR affiliate about the people who make food in Cincinnati. Follow her on Twitter or Instagram: @winemedineme

LESSONS LEARNED FROM JULIE
What caught your attention? What are your takeaways?

38
Jump Into It
By ROBERT MICHAEL ONORATO
Dean of Online Education

How I Got My Start

For many years, I had worked as a part-time college instructor, full-time professor, college administrator, and occasionally in the field of marketing as a business consultant. In the course of all of these different jobs, I had delivered numerous presentations and formally addressed various groups of people many times. But no one had ever paid me specifically for any of these projects—aside from the many courses that I had taught, which is similar to speaking professionally—I guess, but not really the same thing. All of these speaking engagements and opportunities were all just routine and expected parts of these jobs.

Then about 15 years ago, I decided that I wanted to move up to the next step in using my knowledge, background, education, and presentation skills. I decided that I would attempt to offer up this expertise to those outside of my organization and apart from my immediate work network. Of course, the most obvious place to offer my services was at conferences and community events for free, so I started searching for these opportunities.

After several months of searching, I was actually lucky enough to find a potential speaking opportunity for which I would be paid if my proposal was accepted. It was at an educational event in Baltimore, and small but somewhat significant stipends were being offered to a number of selected presenters. I figured out what I thought would be an interesting topic, crafted an attractive title (which is particularly important), and submitted the proposal.

My application was accepted, I traveled to Maryland, and I delivered my first paid presentation. Although I thought the presentation was pretty good at the time, in retrospect, I don't think it was that good at all. The audience did seem to enjoy it; and the people who were hosting the conference thanked me and were supportive and enthusiastic. (They even invited me to future events, for some of which I was compensated.) And to be fair, it wasn't awful, and it probably wasn't even that bad as these things go. (I mean, how many bad presentations at bad conferences have you been to?) But I believe that if one is being paid for a speech, workshop, address, professional development session, or any type of speaking engagement, then one should deliver something that is effective; that is in line with what was requested; that is at least interesting; and if appropriate, entertaining in some way. I suppose that I did minimally meet those requirements. I am confident, though, that I am now a much better presenter and speaker than I was then. Nevertheless, it was a starting point. It was THE starting point.

So, I continued on, soliciting invitations and opportunities to speak at events and workshops and conferences, some of which were paid and some of which were not. Regardless of the opportunity, each one allowed me to practice; experiment; improve; and refine my content, organization, and delivery. This continued on for several years, and probably several dozen speaking engagements. I was then offered a position that consisted almost entirely of delivering presentations. My full-time job was now speaking for money, and I was able to make a living at it and support my family. I continued at this position for more than seven years before moving back into the field of education. However, I still take on the occasional speaking engagement, for which I am happy to say, I still get paid.

My Advice to Aspiring Professional Speakers
After remembering and relating the story of my development into a

paid speaker and presenter, I am tempted to state that the most important piece of advice is simply to jump into it. Just begin and start doing it. Find any opportunity to present your ideas and expertise to an audience even if it is unpaid at first. This will accomplish several things. It will develop your talent, delivery, and professionalism. You will begin to build a network of contacts who are familiar with, and hopefully supportive of, your work. And finally, it will cultivate your reputation as a quality, engaging, and exciting speaker. All of this is important and beneficial. For some, though, the uncertainty of the reaction to one's potential and supposed talents can be a barrier to beginning. However, I think that for many who want to pursue a livelihood such as this, they understand that at some point, they need to just dive in and take that plunge. Some speech or presentation has to be the first one for all of us—for better or worse.

Therefore, I would like to offer a different piece of advice to aspiring professional speakers, and that is this:

Be receptive to feedback and open to change.

Although each of us begins the professional journey with different levels of skill and competency, it is rare to see a public speaker who is truly excellent from his or her first speech or presentation. You should have confidence and believe in yourself, but don't be resistant to hearing about what worked and, more importantly, what didn't work so that you can modify, change, and hopefully improve the next time you speak in public.

In many ways, formally and professionally speaking to others is like a stand-up comedian's act, which is not to say that you want people to laugh at you. You obviously want to be listened to, respected, and taken seriously. But each piece of your speech or presentation is like a comedian's joke. In some ways, each section stands separately as its own individual, though inter-related, unit. Some of these might be effective and successful, and some might not work—just like some of a comedian's jokes might not work. Remember that just because someone doesn't like a part of your presentation or doesn't like the way something was delivered, it doesn't mean that they don't like the content or the session or that they don't like you. Use their feedback—and even their criticism—to grow and improve.

Don't close yourself off from hearing what others have to say about you, your speeches, and your ability. After all, it might not be them; it might be you. In some situations, there might have been a mismatch. Your content and delivery might have been fine, and it might not have been the right crowd for your message; or you were misinformed as to what the audience was expecting. However, you should always reflect on and carefully consider what your friends and audience members tell you. And if that feedback has some merit, change what isn't working. Openly embracing this point of view and this reflection and these actions will more quickly make you a better speaker. And after all, isn't that the path to more work, to working more often, and to getting paid more when you do work?

ABOUT ROBERT

Soon after graduating from the University of Connecticut with a degree in marketing, Robert M. Onorato began an academic career as an adjunct business instructor, moved into academic administration and spent 15 years working as a college administrator in New York State. In time, he returned to the classroom as an adjunct professor, teaching marketing, management, economics, and leadership courses at Sacred Heart University in Fairfield, Connecticut and at Fordham University in New York.

Robert eventually began a public speaking career by delivering presentations and addresses at education and business conferences. These sessions turned into a full-time career when he was hired as a senior professional educator by a major textbook publisher. Here his major responsibilities were creating and providing workshops, training sessions, and conference sessions and addresses. Robert held this position for more than seven years. He now serves as dean of online education at a college in White Plains, New York and still provides the occasional workshop or address.

Robert has earned an MBA from the University of Connecticut and has established Candlewood Consulting. He is also the author of the instructor's resource manual for *Master Student Guide to Academic Success*.

LESSONS LEARNED FROM ROBERT

What caught your attention? What are your takeaways?

39
Sing While You Are Here
By CHEVARA ORRIN
Chief Creative Catalyst

How I Got My Start

I began my journey as a speaker through a love and reverence for the power of words before I had any idea that being a speaker was a viable career or side gig opportunity. As a young girl in elementary school, my teachers often scolded me for "talking too much" in class. I was an avid reader, always had questions, and had been raised to voice my opinion by my politically active and socially justice engaged mom. My mother would take us to school board and city council meetings, protest marches, and educational lectures. I found inspiration in words that transformed community. I grew up hearing the fiery speeches of civil rights leaders and experienced firsthand the compelling oratorical skills that moved crowds to action. As a young professional, fresh from college, I was tasked with presenting to legislators in our nation's capital as I championed for women who were third-generation welfare recipients enrolled in an innovative program to obtain jobs in the skilled-trade industry. With no formal speaking experience, I found myself a few years later serving as a marketing spokesperson for city government in Atlanta. Six years as a university administrator in North Carolina allowed me to explore the possibility of public speaking. I began emceeing galas, speaking at corporate and community events, and presenting lectures at universities throughout the state.

As a social entrepreneur, after founding two nationally recognized campaigns, We Are Straight Allies and #WhiteAndWoke, I decided to become more intentional and focused as a speaker. I researched agencies and applied with CAMPUSPEAK. The organization is recognized as the premiere campus speaker's bureau, and the tools and resources that I've gained have been invaluable. As a diversity, equity, and inclusion practitioner, I speak with organizations across the nation, often about difficult and challenging subject matter: unconscious bias, racial equity, gender parity, LGBTQ+ equality, and sexual harassment in the workplace.

I am filled with the same passion and commitment whether I am standing in front of thousands of students, faculty, and staff at a university speaking about academic success and leadership or engaged with a small group of executives grappling with cultural transformation.

My Advice to Aspiring Professional Speakers

Speak your truth. Find your passion. Believe in your expertise. There is a connection with audiences that is ignited through authenticity. Whatever your journey, however challenging, there is an opportunity to affirm others who may be experiencing a similar path. As a sexual violence survivor, I have learned to embrace the defining moments in my life and share stories that inspire, educate, and empower. Speakers don't have to be academically trained. Life experiences are valuable and can translate into powerful messages. My favorite talk, "I am the Dream of Immigrant and Enslaved" begins as I share the story of my great-grandfathers, Samuel Rutzky and Burrell Bevel. One sailed on the St. Paul from Kiev, Russia and first set foot on American soil in 1902, and the other was born into enslavement and bondage on an Alabama cotton plantation in 1937. Both were seeking freedom.

Create an intimate focus group of friends and colleagues who both share and have differing perspectives. I invite members of my village to speaking engagements when possible and ask for critical feedback. I also record my talks to review so that I can improve.

Recognize that our unique differences make a difference and that speakers come in many forms. We often associate public speaking with "proper diction," "stage presence," "able-bodiedness," and "the professional sector." There are hundreds of motivational speakers that honor the full complexity of who they are. Speakers who are changing the world and influencing public policy after spending decades incarcerated. Speakers who are wheelchair users or who have speech differences that have inspired others to fulfill their possibilities. Speakers who, because of a life-altering experience, are now motivated to share.

I am reminded of a quote by Henry David Thoreau:

Most [people] lead lives of quiet desperation and go to the grave with the song still in them."

Use your voice. Own your power. Sing while you are here.

ABOUT CHEVARA

Chevara Orrin is an award-winning diversity and inclusion practitioner; social entrepreneur; published author; social justice activist; independent filmmaker; and dynamic public speaker signed with nationally recognized speakers bureau, CAMPUSPEAK. She is a forward-thinking catalyst who is passionate about igniting organizational transformation. In her current role as Chief Creative Catalyst for Collective Concepts, she is best known for having conceived and co-created We Are Straight Allies, a national marketing campaign to support equality and move towards the passage of inclusive policies to protect the LGBTQ community and #WhiteAndWoke™, an initiative to raise awareness about racial inequality and promote equity through intentional action. The successful Allies campaign has drawn the participation of prominent figures such as feminist icon Gloria Steinem, gubernatorial candidate Andrew Gillum, Olympic gold medalist and civil rights attorney Nancy Hogshead-Makar; cultural and faith leaders; and superstars from the corporate world including the CEOs of Florida Blue and SunTrust Bank. Chevara is executive producer of an independent documentary, *The Story of Denise*, that premiered at the 2019 Outflix Film Festival in Memphis, Tennessee. The film explores the transgender experience and family acceptance. The Allies campaign was instrumental in the February 14, 2017 passage of a fully comprehensive Human Rights Ordinance in Jacksonville, Florida. Chevara is currently filming *Why is Washington [Still] Burning?* It is a documentary short that chronicles the actions of a collective of 100 white and Jewish activists in support of black rebellions days after Dr. Martin Luther, Jr's assassination. The film explores today's role of white Americans in the struggle for racial justice.

Chevara is deeply inspired by the legacy of her parents. She is the daughter of a white, Jewish mother who served as the lead coordinator for the 1967 March on the Pentagon in opposition of the Vietnam War and a black father who was a top lieutenant of the Rev. Martin Luther King, Jr. and a driving force behind many critical civil rights campaigns of the 1960s, including the 1963 Birmingham Children's Crusade, 1965 Selma to Montgomery March, and the passage of the Voting Rights Act. Her father was portrayed by Grammy and Academy award-winning artist Common in the critically acclaimed film, *Selma*. Chevara is also a survivor of childhood poverty, incest, teenage pregnancy, and domestic violence. It is because of, not in spite of, her personal journey of tragedy and triumph that she is inspired to use her experiences and voice as a catalyst to ignite social transformation.

Chevara's work and passion live at the intersection of gender liberation, racial equity, LGBTQ equality, and arts activism. She is an innovative leader with more than 20 years of experience ranging from senior management in the arts and higher education sectors to consulting with Fortune 500 clients. As a diversity, equity, and inclusion (DEI) strategist, Chevara specializes in devising and facilitating leadership and employee learning sessions on improving cultural agility and work climate, developing comprehensive organizational strategies, building marketplace DEI brand awareness, and developing business resource groups (BRG).

Chevara has served as a member of numerous nonprofit boards including the Greater Fort Lauderdale Chamber of Commerce Women's Council, Cultural Council of Greater Jacksonville's Cultural Services Grants Panel, RiverRun International Film Festival, Atlanta History Center Advisory Council, and the Winston-Salem Symphony. Chevara is a frequent conference presenter, lecturer, and motivational speaker. An outspoken advocate for the eradication of sexual violence against women and girls, Chevara founded WhiteSpace SafeSpace, a monthly support group and forum for incest survivors. She is a contributing author in a recently published anthology, *love WITH accountability* (AK Press, fall 2019), a collection of writings that examine how accountability is a powerful and necessary form of love needed to address child sexual abuse.

Chevara has facilitated workshops and dialogues across the United States from TEDx Jacksonville to serving as keynote speaker for the National Security Agency (NSA) Diversity Speaker Series to co-hosting "Jazz Under the Bridge" with legendary Tony award-winner Ben Vereen. She believes that "There is a human cost when we fail to connect. Ideas unborn. Dreams unrealized. Communities un-ignited."

Chevara has been recognized by the White House and the Human Rights Campaign as a leader, advocate, and ally for the LGBTQ community and has been featured in publications including *The Washington Post, Atlanta Journal-Constitution, Tikkun Magazine* and *The Feminist Wire*. She has also been a featured guest on SiriusXM Radio and highlighted in John Blake's 2007 book *Children of the Movement*, a powerful glimpse into the heart and soul of the Freedom Movement of the sixties as seen by its children. Her numerous awards for community service include the United Nations Association, Broward County Chapter honoree, Hands on Jacksonville Unity in Action award, University of North Florida Woman of Influence, Jacksonville "Who's Who for Justice award, Jacksonville Mayor's Commission on the Status of Women honoree, Girls Inc. Jacksonville "Women of Vision" award, Spelman College Game Changers award, Triad Business Journal "Forty under 40," and Winston-Salem Urban League Community Leader of the Year. Chevara is a 2010 alum of Leadership Winston-Salem and a graduate of Leadership Broward Class XXXVII.

A native of Washington, D.C., Chevara was raised in Memphis, Tennessee and earned a bachelor's degree in mass communication from the University of Memphis. She is a 2017 graduate of Georgetown University's Strategic Diversity and Inclusive Management Program. She is the proud mother of Michael, a graduate of Columbia University and senior trainer with The Posse Foundation, and William, an actor, yogi, and college student in Atlanta, Georgia who is featured in the film *Wait No Longer*, the true story of the 1964 race riots in St. Augustine, Florida.

LESSONS LEARNED FROM CHEVARA

What caught your attention? What are your takeaways?

40
Make the Material Come Alive
By JESSICA M. PIERCE
Founder and CEO, Career Connectors

How I Got My Start

My jump into the professional speaking world was a complete surprise. I was working in corporate operations at a large technology company. During that time, I was offered a promotion into the training department to oversee instructors throughout locations all over the world. After I accepted the position, I had my first one-on-one with my new director, and she let me know that a new piece of my position would be to not only manage the instructors throughout the world but to also train and develop them. This was a complete shock to me—the only presentation I'd ever given was a five-minute update during a staff meeting.

Well, since failure was not an option (I was a single mom, providing the sole income for our little family), I dove full in and learned everything I could about training and presenting. I immediately signed up for a Toastmasters program. The very first presentation for Toastmasters is only three minutes, and the information was a short story about myself. I walked up there, stumbled through it, gave 50 "um's and ah's," and then cried when I was done. I was horrible, but again failure was not an option; so I showed up every single week. As I practiced and began training around the world, it got easier and I got better. I found a love for speaking in front of groups! Thank goodness for that promotion!

My Advice to Aspiring Professional Speakers

My best speaking days are delivering content that I care about deeply. I encourage speakers to find topics that relate to them, a topic in which they can tell a story and connect with the audience. That is often difficult if given material, but there is always a story that relates to the material and to the speaker's life. Find that connection and make the material come alive. People love stories, people connect with stories, and people will trust you when they have that connection.

ABOUT JESSICA

Jessica founded Career Connectors in 2009 after the economy had a personal impact on her family. Originally started as a small volunteer group to help write résumés, it quickly turned into a larger organization helping people get back to work. She is now the CEO of Career Connectors as well as a known speaker, hiring professional, and career transition expert. Career Connectors has now served over 37,000 people in the Phoenix area and has been identified by the *Phoenix Business Journal* as the #4 networking group in the area.

Jessica has spoken at The White House in the Forum on Job Clubs in United States, her focus being on employer engagement. She has also been named as one of Phoenix's 40 Under 40 and is an award recipient of the Arizona Foothill's Women Who Move the Valley. Jessica has been featured in the *Arizona Republic* (PHOENIX, ARIZONA) and on NBC Channel 12, ABC Channel 15, AZ Channel 3, and more.

Jessica has three amazing kids and a wonderful husband who also dedicates his life to getting people back to work. You can often hear them say "Living the dream!"

LESSONS LEARNED FROM JESSICA
What caught your attention? What are your takeaways?

SECTION 4 ACTION PLAN

Based on what you learned from the contributors in this section, what action will you take?

SECTION 5

41
Be Open to Change
By KELLY RADI
Motivational Speaker | Award-Winning Author | Real-Life Wonder Woman

How I Got My Start

I grew my speaking chops as a "spokesmom" for a healthcare system. You read that right! Spokes-MOM. After being an at-home mom for 16 years, I was hired to educate and promote a family health initiative in our region. They wanted a mom-voice and a mom perspective to engage their clientele. What a great way to connect with people while developing my speaking skills!

I eventually left that position to start my own business and write my first book on parenting through the high school-to-college transition. Even though I fancied myself a writer and the book earned awards, I found myself drawn back to speaking as I was asked to speak to parents and students on high school and college campuses about this emotional transition.

Speaking was (and is!) my jam. But I knew I had plenty of room to improve my craft—and I wanted to learn about the *business* of speaking, so I joined the Speaker Academy through the Minnesota chapter of the National Speakers Association (NSA). This academy—like a master's program in speaking—was a game changer for me! I learned not only about platform skills, but how to run a speaking business (sales, negotiations, marketing collateral, and such). And most importantly, it connected me with other professional speakers who care about the integrity and the quality of the speaking industry.

My Advice to Aspiring Professional Speakers

Get involved in a professional speaking group like NSA. Network with other speakers who are honest and ethical, who are lifelong learners, and who are willing to mentor you. And, of course, be a partner. Offer to help others in their speaking journeys.

The other business advice I would offer is be open to change. This is a process, not a destination! You may reinvent yourself as your career, skills, and knowledge base grow. For example, I've now launched a second book called *Wonder-FULL: Activate Your Inner Superpowers (No Cape Required)* and it has become my signature keynote. Because I was open to change (and listened to advice from my trusted mentors), I went from supporting parents through "the college launch" to empowering people so they can live their fullest, most productive lives. And my business has grown exponentially because of this change.

Is speaking an easy career? No. I can honestly say it is the hardest I've ever worked. It requires consistency, patience, thick skin, humility, and persistence. An entrepreneurial spirit is critical.

But is it fulfilling? Absolutely! Knowing the work you do improves someone else's life is truly amazing. It is why we do what we do.

ABOUT KELLY

Kelly Radi is a real-life Wonder Woman.

She motivates and inspires others through real stories, superhero history lessons, and relevant take-aways. Her audiences leave refreshed and confident, armed with new perspectives, and ready to create a life of significance— personally and professionally. After all, superheroes don't just sit there. They take action!

A former spokesperson for a healthcare system, Kelly now collaborates with people in a variety of industries. She consults with both for-profit and non-profit entities including: Delta Air Lines, LeadingAge Minnesota, Women In Aviation, Thrivent Financial, Women in Trucking, Minnesota Department of Human Services, Big Brothers Big Sisters, and several high schools and colleges.

Kelly's award-winning book, *Out To Sea: A Parents' Survival Guide to the Freshman Voyage*, is the go-to resource for parents as they navigate the high school-to-college transition. Her second book, called *Wonder-FULL: Activate Your Inner Superpowers (No Cape Required)*, empowers people to live their fullest, most-productive lives.

Kelly is a member of the National Speakers Association, winning the Minnesota Speaker Academy Award for 2018.

Connect with Kelly at raditowrite.com

LESSONS LEARNED FROM KELLY

What caught your attention? What are your takeaways?

42
Find Your Tribe
By ELAINE SIMPSON
National Speaker | Consultant | Trainer | Author

How I Got My Start

As an identical twin within a set of triplets born on Christmas Day, I had been a relatively quiet but strong-willed individual. I wanted to be different from my twin and struggled to do this until I fell into property management, like most people do, when I was a freshman in college. Ironically, my dad owned a property management company, and I always swore I would not go into property management. Fast forward to my freshman year, and the store at which I worked closed unexpectantly overnight; I was desperate and needed to get a job, so I took a leasing job. This was pivotal in my career and would ultimately impact my future as a speaker on property management and hospitality management. Being a leasing consultant forced me to speak up and show how my product and myself were different from our competition, which taught me how to be different and impactful.

I remained in the business of property management for over 20 years and on numerous occasions, had conversations with, at the time, my boyfriend about starting my own consulting and training business focused on property management but thought it was outside my reach until I was laid off in 2007 due to the downward turn of the economy. I was a single mother with no income and had no idea what I was going to do to support my son and myself when a friend and owner of a property management company needed help with training and creating a leasing and marketing binder … My consulting company, Occupancy Solutions, as well as my speaking career was born.

Twelve years later and I speak not only nationally but have been fortunate to speak at a couple of events in Canada, Puerto Rico, and Mexico. I have since expanded our services and my speaking to include working with hotels on their customer service and enhancing their guests' experiences. Now, Occupancy Solutions provides numerous services to property and hospitality professionals, and I perform numerous keynotes annually; act as an emcee for a number of association award banquets; and provide workshops, programs, and breakout sessions to professionals across the country and beyond.

I have said many times I am fortunate to love what I do and to do what I love! I love speaking to a group and seeing the light bulb go on … it's magical and energizing!

My Advice to Aspiring Professional Speakers
To be successful, one must find his/her tribe and be present within that tribe! I joined the National Speakers Association (NSA) a few years ago and found good information and resources on being a better speaker, and that was good; but it was not all that I needed to be successful. Being an entrepreneur, aka solopreneur, and a speaker can be very lonely in both a professional as well as a personal aspect. Often times, you don't get the full support and understanding from friends and family that you need to start a business and/or speaking career. Finding people in similar situations, experiences, and of like minds and needs can be life changing in a speaking career.
I have been incredibly fortunate to find Power Women a community within NSA. The support, resources, friendship, and energy that we provide each other is incredible and, undeniably, a huge contributor to my success! When I first joined, the people with whom I connected within the group were just other members of the group

to which I belonged, then they became acquaintances, then to friends, and I now feel as though they are my tribe and my family!

This group proved we are family when a couple of years ago, I lost my husband unexpectedly. These ladies circled around me, as a tribe often does, to comfort, protect, and lift me up! They called, visited (in some cases, via a several hours' drive each way), texted, sent cards, and checked in on me as I dealt with the shock and the loss of losing him. A couple of them stepped in and filled in for me at speaking engagements that I had already booked, and not once did any of them hesitate! I strive to be as good to them as they are to me. That is what makes a tribe, so you have to find your own tribe. Surround yourself by those who will step up, be present; support you; and in some cases, provide hugs and wipe away your tears.

ABOUT ELAINE

Elaine founded Occupancy Solutions to provide operations, marketing, sales and leasing, training, and consulting services in the multifamily and hospitality industries throughout the United States.

Occupancy Solutions, LLC has provided services, keynotes, and workshops on property and hospitality management since 1986. Occupancy Solutions assists clients by providing proven, cost-effective techniques and strategies that achieve increased income and reduced vacancies.

Ms. Simpson is a passionate national speaker, consultant, trainer, and author with offices in Detroit, Michigan and Phoenix, Arizona. Her passion for speaking and helping others began early on, and it has stayed with her ever since.

As an identical twin within a set of triplets born on Christmas Day, Elaine has always strived to stand out from the pack and goes above and beyond to create plans, strategies, workshops, trainings, and keynote presentations that are unique, energizing and equally as engaging. Sharing her positive and not so positive stories about being a triplet, possessing 30+ years in property management, and being a seasoned road warrior, Elaine uses her experiences, struggles, successes and stories—the good, bad and the ugly—to connect and relate to anyone who has customers and/or employees. With humor and interactive exercises, Elaine grabs the audience and takes it for a ride that it will enjoy, remember, and from which it will learn. Elaine is on a mission to inspire individuals, teams and their leaders to fully realize the positive impact they have on their residents, guests, each other, and the organizations they build. Elaine is a member of the National Speakers Association; a certified John Maxwell coach, trainer, and speaker; and a National Apartment Association Education Institute Facilitator. Additionally, she is a licensed real estate broker in Michigan and Arizona and a Certified Senior Real Estate Specialist.

LESSONS LEARNED FROM ELAINE

What caught your attention? What are your takeaways?

43
Jump in With Both Feet
By JEANNIE SMITH
Agent of Remarkable Change

How I Got My Start

As a human resources professional, speaking and presenting information was my responsibility at many different companies for which I was either employed or with which I consulted. Connecting with people on both a professional and personal level and helping them to be their best was a lot of what I did.

Over the years, in my quest to continually learn and expand my knowledge, I attended many conferences and events. As I sat in the audience listening to speakers, I thought and questioned, "Would I have said this differently or included that?" It then occurred to me that in asking myself those and many other questions, the bigger question I started asking myself was why I was not the one on the stages? I had a visual over and over again where I was the one providing knowledge and inspiration. I was driven by a force that was leading me to understand my true calling where I soon discovered that I had an abundance of information to share, and I confirmed that others could benefit greatly from me sharing.

I've been told that what I've shared over the years has profoundly changed both business and coaching clients on emotional and mental levels where they then made remarkable professional or personal changes in their lives and within themselves. I've also been told that I help audience members focus on the many opportunities instead of problems all while inspiring them to maximize their potential.

Once I figured out my "why," my "what" was abundantly clear. It became natural for me to start sharing my personal experiences, business knowledge, and leadership skills—my authentic self with larger audiences.

My Advice to Aspiring Professional Speakers

The most important piece of advice I would offer aspiring professional speakers is for them to be authentic. To do this, they should connect with themselves, recognize their "whys," and commit to be their authentic selves in everything they do. Over the span of my career, I've interacted with so many individuals who do what they do for reasons other than those that support them being themselves. I can't emphasize enough how important it is to be YOU. It's important to realize that your authenticity is the one thing—more than anything else—that makes you unique. I have found that what captures other people's attention and leaves an impression is being your unique remarkable self. Aspiring professional speakers should share their own experiences—those things that make them unique. All too often too many folks pretend to be someone else. It's important to embody your own uniqueness and identity.

Most people spend so much of their time conforming to those around them that they miss opportunities right in front of them to be themselves. Surprisingly, going along with what everybody else is doing is also the one thing that makes us unnoticeable. When we conform with the crowd, it makes us just like everyone else. It leaves nothing noteworthy or remarkable about us. This is often a tough situation because our identity shifts from being our authentic self to being what everyone else wants us to be. If you truly want to make a professional speaking difference and be remarkable, then you must first learn how to be yourself and live authentically with a deep sense of who you are, why you do what you do, and what you have to offer.

To leave an impression on those to whom we speak, we must be secure in our authenticity and speak from the heart. This begins with our inner thoughts. When you can take charge of the thoughts and feelings that control your mind and replace them with those that positively support YOUR true intention, you begin to understand your values and feelings of worth.

Know that all decisions are choices, and you are free to make those that support your authentic self. To make choices that are authentic to your true self, you must first have a firm grasp of who your true self is. When I coach leaders in this area, I always point them back to their values. Our values are what drive all our life's decisions. Values are a reflection of what's important to you and a short-hand way of describing your motivations. Together with your beliefs, values are the factors that drive your decision making.

When you decide to follow your own path, you will look, feel, and ARE different from everyone else. Your authenticity is the one thing that will make you remarkable in every way. When you live authentically true to yourself, you will have the confidence to jump in with both feet rather than sit on the sidelines wondering if it might be a good idea—GO FOR IT!

ABOUT JEANNIE

Jeannie Smith is president of HR-Rx, Inc., https://www.HR-Rx.com, a coaching and consulting firm where she has a proven track record of helping individuals and teams be their best and live remarkable lives. Jeannie partners with leaders at all levels to understand what is keeping them from achieving their goals and to increase their value by energetically building a new strategic perspective and approach to making deliberate remarkable choices. By focusing on maximizing communication, engagement, and efficiency for individuals and teams, integrating effective processes, programs and practices, she helps individuals and organizations to be more efficient and to maintain a strong competitive advantage.

Jeannie is a certified leadership coach, professional speaker, and human development consultant. She has over 25 years of combined experience in positions of human resources generalist, manager, director, executive, inspirational speaker, coach, and consultant with both public and private organizations in medical device and practice, pharmaceuticals, communications, real estate, public broadcasting, security/anti-theft, education, software development, and other high-tech industries. She holds a Master of Science in Human Resource Management from Chapman University and a Bachelor of Arts in Public Administration from San Diego State University. Jeannie is certified as a Senior Professional in Human Resource Management in California from the HR Certification Institute and holds a Senior Certified Professional Certificate from the Society for Human Resource Management (SHRM). Jeannie has completed the Institute for Professional Excellence in Coaching's comprehensive, accredited coaching training program and is certified as a Professional Coach and a Master Practitioner on the Energy Leadership Index Assessment.

Fulfilling her passion to help individuals be their best and live remarkable lives, Jeannie has taken to the stage to share her decades of personal experience, business knowledge, and leadership skills with diverse audiences. Jeannie speaks on topics of communication, connection, leadership, and mindset. Her mission is to increase employee engagement by partnering with individuals and corporations to create value-based cultures and to maximize human potential.

LESSONS LEARNED FROM JEANNIE
What caught your attention? What are your takeaways?

44
Surround Yourself With Titans, Not Titanics
By DR. JIM SMITH, JR. CSP
President and CEO, Jim Smith Jr. International

How I Got My Start

My journey into the speaking business has been filled with many twists and turns. After nine years in corporate, initially as a copywriter in the marketing department then as a trainer in the human hesources department, I discovered my love of training, speaking, and coaching. During this time, I began to believe that I was just as skilled as many of the vendors that were hired to come in and share their learning and development programs. However, one such vendor blew me away with his poise, wit, creativity, and subject matter expertise. During a break in his diversity and inclusion workshop, I introduced myself and asked if we could connect after the workshop.

We did, and that eventually led to him hiring me as a part-time subcontractor facilitator. I still maintained my full-time position. My manager, at the time, gave her blessing and let me work a four-day work week or take personal days whenever I facilitated a training session for him. I enjoyed plenty of success and gained a ton of valuable experience. After working internally for two organizations up to that point, it was my initial time taking my speaking and training skills to organizations where people didn't know me. I fell in love! I knew that this is what I wanted to do full-time. I shared my dream with my manager, and she began to coach me in that vein while still supporting me with the work that I was doing for our organization.

I eventually moved onto another full-time role with another organization—my daughter was born, and I needed to shorten my commute; I became vice president of the Business Learning Resources department with my new employer. Nevertheless, I continued doing subcontract work. My role in my new organization was short-lived as we were acquired by another organization. I was able to convince my current leadership team to provide me with a severance package (six months' salary and six months' benefits). Immediately following this, I started work with two other consulting firms (with one, I was doing diversity and inclusion work and with the other, professional trainer development). After four years of this, I started my own company and begin my pursuit of becoming a full-time speaker and trainer. It's been 17 years, and I'm still going strong. I have spoken in 25 plus countries and 43 states. I've authored three books and co-authored another. I'm recognized as a Certified Speaking Professional (CSP), a designation that only approximately 15 percent of the speakers in the country have. It's been some journey, and I don't plan on retiring any time soon if ever!

My Advice to Aspiring Professional Speakers

I would advise aspiring speakers to: 1. Create a sound business and marketing plan at the outset; 2. Understand their "why" for what they do; 3. Be their authentic selves and not let others' opinions of them become their reality; 4. Develop their personal brand; and 5. Surround themselves with Titans, not Titanics.

ABOUT DR. JIM

For over 20 years, hundreds of thousands of people, both national and international audiences of all sizes, have experienced the passion, creativity, storytelling, unshakeable positivity, and mind-shifting power of Dr. Jim Smith, Jr. CSP. Dr. Jim is a lightning rod in the professional and personal development spaces, creating performance breakthroughs for organizations, teams, breakthroughs for organizations, teams and individuals looking to improve in the areas of communication, authenticity, personal power, leadership, presentation and/or facilitation skills.

After 14 years in corporate America and four years working with several training and development and diversity and inclusion consulting firms, Dr. Jim formed Jim Smith Jr. International to help others remove self-created barriers and **jump into their BIGNESS**. He says that he "disrupts ordinary." His mother, Nanci Smith; twelfth grade high school teacher, Mrs. Brodie; former manager at the Vanguard Group, Kathy Cook; and little league baseball coach, Sam Gallman fueled his motivational spirit, and he continues to fuel others.

A personal-power expert and transformational speaker, trainer, and coach, Dr. Jim has started a "no excuses personal accountability" revolution. He does this through in-house workshops, public boot camps, best-selling books, blogs, coaching, and motivational keynotes. Those who have been JIMPACTed say that he has the rare ability to walk the line between direct and encouraging. His teaching and coaching methods have worked regardless of the industry or the country.

Dr. Jim has taken his message to over 25 countries and has taught presentation skills for the Rutgers University Executive and International Executive MBA Programs since 2008. In addition, he has worked with and coached speakers, trainers, and television and radio personalities in how to make compelling, engaging, and "game-changing" presentations. He has achieved the National Speakers Association (NSA) Certified Speaking Professional designation—a designation that only about 17 percent of NSA members worldwide have earned. His clients include Biogen, Sabic (Saudi Arabia), Accenture, Aflac, Genentech, Jockey, Comcast, KenCrest, The Kimmel Center for Performing Arts, Tweezerman, The American Club (Singapore), Celgene, Western Union, Aimco, Genworth Financial, Medtronic, Metlife, and Lockheed Martin.

Dr. Jim has authored three books with his last, ***The No Excuse Guide to Success: No Matter What Your Boss or Life Throws at You,*** earning an NAACP Image Award nomination. His Jim's Journal blog reaches audiences all over the world. When he's not JIMPACTing, Dr. Jim serves on the board of Variety, the Children's Charity and helps to raise awareness and support for people on the autism spectrum.

LESSONS LEARNED FROM DR. JIM

What caught your attention? What are your takeaways?

45
Do the Work and Don't Go It Alone
By TISH TIMES
CEO and Founder, Tish Times Networking and Sales Training

How I Got My Start

Before I started speaking, I was hosting networking events and connecting people. As the host, I was frequently in the front of the room, and I think my attendees just assumed I was a professional speaker. I really wasn't. By word of mouth, people started contacting me to speak for their organizations, and eventually, I was asked to be a keynote speaker for a large event. I over-prepared and was so nervous I thought I'd wet myself! My sweet husband came to support me for my first "real speaking gig." Poor thing. He tried to be encouraging when I asked him how I did. I'd talked in circles and probably confused the whole audience! I had no idea what I was doing. I had tried to fit into the box of what I thought a speaker should be. I totally abandoned who I was and left behind the magic that others saw in me when I was running my events. Once I figured out that it was okay to be myself and that my authenticity was my brilliance, it really clicked for me. Soon after that realization, I was invited to speak at a very large conference. Though still nervous, I walked on stage and found my home. Early on, I realized the need to develop my skill, so I started connecting with other speakers. I hired a coach, and I joined groups to find speaking opportunities. Although I've been speaking professionally now for almost a decade, I still recognize how important it is to continue to hone my skills and stay relevant. For me, speaking is a calling. It is my happy place. I am so honored that I get to share my life and experience with the world—often from a stage.

My Advice to Aspiring Professional Speakers

To aspiring speakers, I would say:

- Be less of a "speaker/presenter" and more of a conversationalist. If you speak to your audience as though you really care about what they need, truly connect, and be more vulnerable in your talks, you will be more likely to have an opportunity to continue the conversation in the form of more business.

- Do the work. Practice with and without an audience. Practice in front of a mirror. Record yourself. Ask for feedback. Make corrections and practice more.

- Don't forget speakers speak. That means you should find and create opportunities to speak. Something I did early on was to have free events at the public library. I would put an ad in the paper, (now you would probably do it online), create my "signature talk," and basically practice on the 10 or 15 people who would show up! Additionally, I created Google alerts with "speaking opportunities" as the search term to find places to speak. When you do this, you can get daily emails that provide you places where you can apply to speak.

- Hone your craft so you can get paid for it! Make sure your talk is engaging, meets a need, and is memorable.

- Believe in yourself. I know how it feels to get in front of a group and doubt everything that I am about to say. Conversely, I know how it feels to speak with conviction, know that what I am saying is making an impact, and to believe that my words change lives. No one will believe until you do. As you are honing your craft, you must simultaneously do self-development. You must develop your self-confidence and trust that you have something your audience needs.

- Hire help. My speaking went to another level when I got a coach. You'd be surprised how an expert can pull magic out of you. Don't go it alone.

ABOUT TISH

Tish Times is the founder of Tish Times Networking and Sales. Tish is also a certified networker; community builder; and franchise owner for Network in Action in Phoenix, Arizona. For nearly 10 years, Tish has been teaching small businessowners, solo entrepreneurs, and sales professionals to increase income with unparalleled sales and networking strategies. Tish empowers sales professionals to create revenue-generating business connections, follow-up effectively, stay top-of-mind, shorten the sales cycle, and close sales with ease.

Tish's books include *Networking is Not a One-Night Stand - A Guide for Building Lasting Business Relationships*, *The Unstoppable Confidence Networking Playbook,* and *10 Super Simple Networking Steps for Career Success*. Most recently, Tish has developed the Unstoppable Confidence Sales Academy, a business school that teaches a systematic, sincere, and effective approach to networking and sales to produce lucrative bottom-line results.

You can find her at www.TishTimes.com or contact her at tish@tishtimes.com
www.facebook.com/coachtishtimes
www.twitter.com/tishtimes
www.linkedin.com/in/tishtimes

LESSONS LEARNED FROM TISH

What caught your attention? What are your takeaways?

46
What You Are Doing is FUN!
By ANDRÉ van HALL
The Curiosity Instigator

How I Got My Start

It all started, like it does for so many of us—a life changing event.

On August 15, 2011, when I woke up, I realized something was off with my eyesight. Many tests later, the verdict was in. I would be blind in two weeks. While the diagnosis was scary, I felt secure in my job. I was the CEO of a 130-year-old institution; I had achieved awesome results, even through the recession thanks to a fabulous team. That same team is the one that wrote to the board that it would pick up the slack in the areas where sight was necessary. Needless to say, I was shocked and dismayed, when a year later, I was let go. Not only was I adjusting to my new reality, but now the security of my job was gone.

By then, I was 59 years old, so you can imagine the insurmountability of finding a job in the hospitality industry. To complicate things, I refused to have to relocate one more time and have to learn a new city as a blind man. I could not find a job.

It was then that I decided that a speaking career would truly motivate me. I had chaired several boards, emceed events, and spoken to large groups. So, launching a speaking career would be truly, truly easy, right?

I learned that, of course, I would first have to pick a subject, but the subject could not be so broad as to not clearly define what "problem I solve." The obvious choice was to speak on service; I had worked at two of the top 10 hotels in the world, and some of the largest, too.

So service came to me naturally. But I could not get motivated to do that. I wanted to affect middle and upper managers who, in turn, could affect larger groups of people.

Having had to adjust to 12 moves in three continents, two marriages, and blindness, I thought I was a natural to speak on CHANGE. So I decided to do so. But, from attending the Colorado Speakers Academy, I learned that picking something as broad as change would make it hard to stand out in a field of hundreds of speakers who also spoke on change. After exhaustive research, I decided to narrow the field by linking CURIOSITY as the catalyst for change.

I prepared my speech and declared myself ready. How wrong I was!

My Advice to Aspiring Professional Speakers

Here is a minimal list of the things you will need to do to begin to claim that you are a speaker:

1. Have good video of you presenting
2. Have good photography
3. Create great content for your website
4. Create your website
5. Get testimonials in video and in writing from groups to which you speak
6. Join National Speakers Association (NSA) and Toastmasters to continually grow in your mastery of speaking
7. Get involved in such groups as Meeting Professionals International (MPI), American Society of Association Executives (ASAE), and other groups that hire speakers for their conferences
8. Speak, speak and speak, to rotary and other service clubs, perform free talks, and talk to friends
9. Create business cards
10. Continuously search for paid speaking opportunities

11. Join or form a "mastermind" group to help you with feedback, accountability, and support
12. Write blogs to post on your website and to offer to organizations where you will speak
13. Refine and update your presentation
14. Make yourself "visible" in your community of influence so people are reminded of your services
15. Speak, speak, and speak to any group to test what works and what needs revision

Okay, so the above is truly a brief list of things to accomplish before you get started and to succeed once you do. It will require money, a source of income other than speaking while you transition, and tons of patience … and an understanding that what you are doing … is FUN!

I have heard it said that "speaking is a hard way to make an easy living." And realize that about 80% of speakers don't make enough from their speaking business to live off of it.

ABOUT ANDRÉ

A native of Argentina, André, has worked at some of the most prestigious hotels in the world to include the Hotel Vier Jahreszeiten in Hamburg (once recognized as a top 10 hotel in the world), the Ritz in Paris, and the St. Regis in New York. Additionally, he has managed some of the largest hotels including the Hyatt Regency in Atlanta and the Adam's Mark in Denver. Before retiring, he was the CEO of the historic Denver Athletic Club. A graduate of the school of Hotel Administration at Cornell University, van Hall has held such positions as director of quality, executive assistant manager, rooms executive, general manager, professor of HR, and CEO. His volunteer activity has afforded him the opportunity to serve on boards of chambers of commerce, United Way, convention and visitors bureaus, rotary clubs, Urban League, and many others.

After suddenly losing his eyesight in late 2011, he started a new career as a professional speaker with an emphasis on motivation, change management, and staff development.

André is an avid cyclist, completing Ride the Rockies, a 450-mile ride over the Rockies, seven times. He also skis, cooks, and has recently completed a book entitled *The Curiosity of Change: How to Bring Light to the Dark Side of Change.*

LESSONS LEARNED FROM ANDRÉ

What caught your attention? What are your takeaways?

47
You Are Never Going to Feel Ready—Do It Anyway
By KYIRA WACKETT, MS, LPC
Therapist | Speaker | Coach | Artist Owner/Founder of Adversity Rising, LLC and Kinda Kreative, LLC

How I Got My Start

I wanted to become a speaker for years. Most of my work, in the beginning, was in leading trainings and workshops or speaking on behalf of organizations and roles I worked in/for. But as I thought about leaping into the world of professional speaking and owning my own business, I was paralyzed by fear and self-doubt. I spent years telling myself that I had to learn more on a given topic or have more credentials to speak on "X." In fact, I talked myself out of starting my own speaking business for over five years. I needed to learn more, be more, do more. "More" continued to be the operative word. But over time, I learned that "more" was just another facet of shame. If all I ever chase is "more," then there is never a time for "enough."

After that, I set a meeting with an organization in my community that was well-respected for putting together awesome workshops and presentations and that vetted and helped promote speakers. An email. That was all it took. When we sat down, I asked about auditioning for the organization and hosting a workshop. I pitched some topics and a timeline for me to speak in about six months. They were on board with me speaking, but instead of six months from now, they had a couple of slots in FOUR WEEKS and pushed me to shift my timeline up much sooner, noting "Sometimes we just have to start." They would help me market and fine-tune anything I needed to. All I had to do was show up and deliver. It was FRIGHTENING.

Suddenly, this thing I wanted was potentially going to happen and all in a matter of weeks. After spending the next few hours trying to talk myself out of speaking, I turned back to a book by Elizabeth Gilbert, *Big Magic*, and was reminded that in that moment, my fear was trying to protect me by keeping me from being vulnerable but that I have the power to work with it rather than succumb to it and help it understand that I would be okay when I stood on stage.

When the night arrived, there were maybe six people in the audience. Thoughts of it not being enough or worrying they would leave immediately filled me. I think I shook on and off the whole session. And did the people leave? No. Did they heckle me? No. Did I get it perfect? Absolutely not. But at the end of my talk, I had accomplished it—my first talk as an independent speaker. The audience applauded and stayed for a while to talk more about the issues raised in the talk. I felt connected to each and every one of them, and that motivation to bring these conversations to the table fueled me.

After that, it wasn't easy, but I had already ripped off the Band-Aid, and so the goal was just to keep doing it. I worked with this company, local libraries, any place you could rent space for free and just started using social media to promote the events and get people to come. After about six months, I started to get a following. What was six became 10 and then became 20, and suddenly I would have 40 to 50+ people at workshops—many of whom became regulars. From there, I started making connections with people and organizations. I started getting offered the opportunity to do paid speaking events. I would receive proposal requests, and the world of speaking professionally (and getting paid for it) was suddenly one I no longer longed to be in but was existing inside of.

My Advice to Aspiring Professional Speakers

You are never going to feel "ready." Fear, shame, and self-doubt are always going to show up when you decide to take the leap to start off in your career. Recognize it and do it anyway.

Your job is not to be perfect. Your job is to just show up and be authentic. My husband once told me, "You already know your topic. That is not what matters. When you speak, all people need is a connection. The rest happens on its own." I like to remind myself (and often others) that I am not saying anything they couldn't find elsewhere. It is not about what I say but the fact that I can present it in a way they may be able to connect with and receive it. For example, I speak on topics such as shame, fear, and communication. There are big names in the field talking about these things—Brené Brown, Mel Robbins, etcetera. I told myself for a long time I could not speak on these topics because "X" was already doing it and doing it better. I was then hired to give a talk on shame for a mental health agency—exploring the way it shows up for clinicians and patients—and on stage, I acknowledged the role shame played in my giving the talk and feeling like a poser or an imposter. After the talk, someone came up to me and thanked me for being so vulnerable and for being willing to show up in spite of that as this was the first time they were really able to connect with and truly understand these higher level concepts. They connected with me. What I had to say may have been the same things as other household names. That was not the point. I did not need to be better or "the best." I simply needed to show up authentically and allow people to connect with me and my story.

Expect rejection. It is not personal. It is just an opportunity to keep growing, evolving, and fine-tuning your work. It is also an opportunity to hone in on your audience and the work you really want to be doing!

ABOUT KYIRA

Kyira Wackett is an artist, public speaker, and community advocate. She holds a master's degree in counseling psychology and is a licensed therapist specializing in eating disorders, anxiety disorders, and trauma.

Kyira has been speaking on topics related to mental health, authenticity, and personal and professional development for over 10 years with a focus on assertive communication, shame, and fear and moving from a life of "busy" to "fulfilled." She brings a unique blend of didactic and hands-on learning to all sessions and believes in empowering people to take the "next right step" for themselves and write the story they want to exist within. In 2017, her company received an America's Small Business Award about which Kyira notes she is still in shock but has used to remind herself every day about how important the work is that she is doing.

LESSONS LEARNED FROM KYIRA

What caught your attention? What are your takeaways?

48
Be Hopeful, Be Bold, Be Fearless, Be You
By CAMILLE R. WALLACE
Founder and CEO of The Culture Company | The Culture Queen

How I Got My Start

I grew up in a home where expectations were high, and the ability to articulate my thoughts, advocate for myself and others, and intelligently communicate were often cultivated and sharpened within me.

Some of my earliest childhood memories include my mother preparing my siblings and me for church presentations. You know— the presentations around the holidays where every child, whether they wanted to participate or not, had a speaking part.

While many of the other children were able to read their speeches from the microphone, my mother insisted that we recite ours from memory every year. In the days leading up to the presentations, I would grow frustrated with her as she made me repeat the lines over and over until I no longer questioned myself or the message. But it wasn't enough to be able to recite the words. No. My beloved mother insisted that I always use expression or, as she would say, "with Exxxxxxppppprrrreeeeeessssssssiiiiiiooooonnnn." as she demonstrated through the roll of her tongue and inflection rising in her voice.

The day of church presentations, after prayer, I would wait my turn, watching as little Jimmy read his lackluster speech. When my turn came, I recall the bundle of nerves growing inside my stomach as I began to recite what I knew to be true. The nerves would subside, and my confidence would grow as the congregation would engage me through call and response. Even now, I can remember feeling how the energy in the room grew each time I emphasized or drove home a talking point.

Through these humble beginnings, I identified a passion place for influencing and impacting others through my speaking.

Over the years, I have found the invaluable public speaking lessons that I learned as a child are transferable in my speaking business today. I have cultivated my craft through advanced education and certifications and through studying my area of expertise until I feel I have mastered the material and can deliver the messages with credibility and conviction. I have learned that effective communication is two-sided—that there's more to speaking than being able to speak the words but rather being able to resonate with those who are listening.

And while I still get "bubble guts" before speaking, I have learned to harness my energy, say a prayer, then deliver my message "with Exxxxxxppppprrrreeeeeesssssssiiiiiiooooonnnn."

My Advice to Aspiring Professional Speakers
Just say it.

Whatever the message you have been assigned to speak—speak fearlessly.

Everyone has a story. You have a story. You have a story that needs to be told. You have a story that needs to be heard. It's not selfish. It's empowering.

If you are questioning the relevance of your message or downplaying the need to share your experience, then don't.

If you are doubting the significance of your story. stop that.

Whether you are speaking to a dozen people in a breakout workshop or to a crowded auditorium—speak fearlessly and wholeheartedly every time, knowing that someone in the crowd is listening, waiting, and needing you to share your message in order to move him/her forward.

The world is waiting on your testimony. We only get to live that experience with you if you share it with us. Many will find in your message of possibility strength to progress. Many will find encouragement by seeing themselves in you. Be confident and believe that your speaking is falling on good ground. Your message is sowing a seed that will bear good fruit in the future. Your voice is nourishing and necessary.

While I am confident that you are a captivating and fabulous speaker, the reality is every message will not reach every listener. I am reminded of the Biblical parable that speaks of the farmer and the seed found in Luke 8: 4-15.

> The farmer began to sow seeds on the ground. Some of the farmer's seed fell on the hard ground where the seed just lay on top of the dirt. Some of the farmer's seed fell on ground that was rocky underneath. Some seed fell among thorny plants. Some seed fell on rich, soft soil. As you can imagine, while the same seed was scattered in various conditions, only the seed that was sown in the ready conditions took root.

This is often the case when we speak. Likewise, the condition of a person's heart will determine if he/she is able to openly receive your message or not. Be prepared to not resonate with everyone, and remember that's okay, too!

Your story connects you to your audience. Because it belongs to you, it is your area of expertise. Own it. Your story builds the foundation for the ideas that you share. Embrace it, and go ahead, and say it!

Be authentic. Be transparent. Be hopeful. Be bold. Be fearless. Be you.

ABOUT CAMILLE

The Culture Queen, Camille R. Wallace, is the founder and CEO of The Culture Company. Camille holds a master's degree in human resource development and a bachelor's degree in legal studies. With over 10 years of experience, Camille combines training, experience, and extensive people development skills to transform professionals into the best versions of themselves.

Her complex roles in corporate sales, professional development, and diversity and inclusion position here to provide support in the areas of executive leadership, talent development, new hire experience, career development, and coaching.

Camille is certified as a leadership coach through Harvard University and is a skilled facilitator and organizational development consultant who is passionate about helping people and organizations develop in meaningful ways that reveal their potential.

LESSONS LEARNED FROM CAMILLE

What caught your attention? What are your takeaways?

49
Never Let Anyone Stop You
By SAMANTHA R. WHITE
Your Christian Mindset Educator

How I Got My Start

I started in the speaking business after so much trouble and heartache were raging in my life. I was raped by my former pastor, beaten by a former husband, and then persecuted by my former church. This pain almost consumed me. I was bitter, broken, and living in a world full of pain. There was not much support for me in my life. I struggled with suicide and self-harm and so many other interpersonal struggles. I turned that pain into a testimony, and I have been spreading the gospel of Jesus Christ ever since. I have also been able to minister to so many women that have been in some of the same situations. Life is not always fair, but we must press on! Honestly, I have been pressing for a while now and I am too far to turn back now! Press on with me.

My Advice to Aspiring Professional Speakers

My mission has sparked the passion in me and has allowed me to overcome so many fears and tribulations as I press towards my true calling. You can do the same by taking the leap of faith and moving towards your destiny. Trouble truly does not last always, and you can move out of that trouble towards peace by taking the leap of faith in the right direction. Continue to move forward, keep the faith, and continue to perfect your God-given talents. Elohim gives you talents and gifts into which we must grow. Think about this: if His plan for your life was easy to accomplish where you do not have any trials, and everything is smooth like plant-based butter (vegan joke), then everyone would be done early, and we may live to only the age of 12. The fact is life has rough and good patches, and we must take the bad with the good and move forward. We simply cannot be like Lot's wife. When she stopped and looked back against the angels' warnings, she became a pillar of salt. Keep pressing toward your mark and let nothing separate you from the love of Christ. My important piece of advice is NEVER let anyone stop you from what the Lord has planned for your life. You will do great things, hunni! Keep the faith :) Email me if you need help— Findpeace@consultpositivity.com!

ABOUT SAMANTHA

Born in North Carolina in a town so small it had just one streetlight at the time, yet the story of Samantha was— even then— written by fate to be so big it was worth sharing with the world! Designed by the maker of all things in such a way that she would live on both lanes of life, Samantha was being propped by God to be able to speak with authority and bring healing to the broken the way she is doing now.

A social innovator and community mobilizer, Samantha was prepared by her experiences in life to be able to confidently carry the message of hope and productivity, which she now teaches. Born into a Christian home with an amazing family of three siblings (two adopted), Samantha was just one happy child learning about the ways of life and about God. But what looked to be a roller-coaster of a perfect childhood and communion with God was soon cut abruptly short by a betrayal so deep it reversed the trajectory of Samantha's life, throwing her into the other lane—a lane of turmoil, wandering, and loss of focus.

Raped by her own pastor at 16, Samantha lost her faith in God and the focus that was hitherto her life. She became an atheist and got intertwined in an emotionally and physically abusive marriage. Battered and wearied by her travails, Samantha roamed about but not for long as she took heed and encountered the manifestation of the promise of God in Matthew 11:28, which invites us to: "Come to me, all you who are weary and burdened and I will give you rest"!

Samantha took the outstretched hands of God and made an important decision to divorce her abusive husband and return to Christ. This would prove to be the defining moment in her life. Today, Samantha is reaping the fruits of that decision and living out the promises of God in Proverbs 10:22 that "the blessings of the Lord makes a person rich and he adds no sorrows with it."

Now married to a supportive husband who pushes her to make greater impact, Samantha is the founder of Consult Positivity, which teaches Christian womenprenuers of color how to lead happy and productive lives. She harnesses the stories of her life and the lessons learned from living on both sides of life to assist others to make the best choices. She knows that God let her past the down times in order to teach her compassion, empathy, and love as well as empower her to lift others, getting them to be happier and more productive.

Her organization teaches Christian womenpreneurs of color how to lead happy and productive lives. She has used her platform to help over 45,000 women and is expanding the reach of her message through her online courses that address how Christian womenprenuers can become happy and productive.

LESSONS LEARNED FROM SAMANTHA

What caught your attention? What are your takeaways?

50
Tell a Story, Be Comfortable, and Be Confident
By TERRI BROUSSARD WILLIAMS
Founder, MovementMakerTribe

How I Got My Start

I have to admit I've been comfortable speaking most of my life. In high school, I was a part of our speech and debate team as well as a teen reporter for our local television station. I would get checked out of school each week to create a news story all on my own. Shortly after high school graduation, you could find me as the mistress of ceremonies for the Alpha Kappa Alpha Sorority, Incorporated debutante ball. I believe it was these small moments that took away any jitters or nervousness that many speakers get when they begin in the business.

As a young professional, others would see this skill in me and put it to use. I was often asked to speak at events for the nonprofits where I served as a board member. Yet, I never owned my gift or thought about monetizing it. Two things would prompt a shift in the way I thought about professional speaking.

An acquaintance worked at the State Bar Association and was hiring speakers for an upcoming conference, and she asked me to speak. I blew it off and thought that I could never say anything that was entertaining nor speak for 20 minutes. And why would she PAY me? I chuckle on the inside every time I think of that moment today!

While serving on a committee for a capital campaign, our consultant asked me to speak to a group and ask everyone assembled to make a financial contribution. I'd done it several times before and wanted to allow someone else to have the opportunity to do the same, so I said "no." She finally talked me into it, and I spoke at a meeting. It was pretty awful! Mostly because my heart wasn't in it that day. I was truly worried that the members of the organization thought that I wanted to speak to have the limelight. When I sat down, she looked at me and said, "What is up with you today? That was so surface." I shared with her that I didn't want to speak because I felt that others should get a chance. She responded by pulling out her laptop and showing me data of how many campaign donations were made when I made the pitch versus when someone else did. I'm a data person, so seeing how I was making an impact shifted my perspective.

This was one of the moments that opened my eyes to see that what I said could not only make a difference, but it could inspire others to think bigger! I could be a leader who could turn a moment into a movement.

Within that year, I spoke on 62 occasions for free and then met Adam Smiley Poswolsky, the author of *The Breakthrough Speaker*. I attended a dinner where he shared what individuals needed to do to begin a speaking career. As he ran through the checklist of what is needed to get started, I had everything but a website and an LLC.

That was in 2016, and the rest is history. What's been most fun is that several people at the dinner where Smiley spoke now have speaking businesses, and we all support each other along the way.

My Advice to Aspiring Professional Speakers
I always get asked what is the number one piece of advice that I have for those getting started. I don't have just one thing but three: tell a story, be comfortable, and be confident. Don't over-prepare your business; just do it. I felt like I had to have everything in place

before I got started, but I had all of the things I needed inside of me. Having a blog, a website, or a podcast didn't make me a speaker; it gave me a platform.

Having a story that I could tell with passion is what made me a speaker. Speakers are brought in by organizations to educate, entertain, or inspire. By simply standing on a stage in front of others, you are instantly an authority, and people are listening to YOU. They want to know that you are human, that you can get up when you are down, and that you are authentic. No matter what it is that you want to share with others through your talks, think about your life—your successes, failures, and lessons learned. Those stories are what set you apart from other speakers and are what make you interesting. Take each of those moments and use them to make the points about your talk. The more you talk about your life, the more authentic you'll be, and quite honestly, it is more likely that you won't be nervous or think about the size of your audience. You'll simply be giving them an update about yourself!

The one thing you do want to spend time on is your branding. It will bring your story to life and make it marketable. I've branded my talks around my root belief: "Leaders turn moments into movements." Any talk I give can fall under that theme, and it's led me to opportunities that I never imagined because it comes from the heart and is concise. I tend to wear the same thing in different colors or the same color when I speak. Not only does it make things look cohesive in my pictures or video for sizzle reels, it helps me cut down on decisions the day of a talk. Most importantly, I know I'll be comfortable in my own skin. It's so important to feel comfortable on stage because not only will it make for a great picture, but it'll help you to be confident. And being confident ensures that you will nail it on stage.

ABOUT TERRI

Terri Broussard Williams believes leaders turn moments into movements. Throughout her accomplished career as an author, broadcast journalist, press secretary for a US Senate Candidate, philanthropist, and lobbyist, Williams has turned public and community service into a professional art-form that has positively impacted millions of lives. For nearly 16 years, Terri made the American Heart Association (AHA) her career home. Her journey at this notable organization sparked her dream of creating significant, community-shifting outcomes. She counts some of the pieces of legislation passed as some of her most distinguished accomplishments, including the Louisiana Smoke-Free Air Act, a game-changing career milestone she experienced at the flourishing age of 28. Broussard Williams received her bachelor's degree from Louisiana State University and is also a graduate of the Social Impact Strategy Executive Education Program at the University of Pennsylvania and holds a graduate certificate in diversity and inclusion from Cornell University. She is currently a graduate student at the University of Pennsylvania, studying Non-Profit Leadership and is expected to graduate in May 2020. She has served on several boards including the Austin Area Urban League, the Annette Strauss Institute for Civic Engagement, the University of Texas McCombs School of Business Capstone Advisory Board, Louisiana State University National Diversity Advisory Board, and the Association of Junior Leagues International among others. In addition to her day job as a tech lobbyist, Terri is focused on paying it forward—encouraging and building up others who strive to create meaningful and groundbreaking change through her blog, movementmakertribe.com. Get to know more about this #firestarter at terribwilliams.com.

LESSONS LEARNED FROM TERRI
What caught your attention? What are your takeaways?

SECTION 5 ACTION PLAN

Based on what you learned from the contributors in this section, what action will you take?

Acknowledgments

We greatly appreciate the following contributors for offering their stories of how they got their starts in the professional speaking business. The advice they gave to rock stars who want to up-level their speaking businesses is invaluable.

Stacy Bernal
Speaker; Author; Coach; and Disruptor at See Stacy Speak, LLC

Brian Biro
America's Breakthrough Coach, Professional Speaker, and Best-Selling Author

Brian Bogert
President/Owner of The Brian Bogert Companies, LLC

Debbie Boone
President of 2 Manage Vets, LLC

Katrina Brittingham, JCDC, JCTC
Chief Executive Coach

Lori Bruhns
Professional Productivity Speaker and Coach

David Bryson
Speaker and Host of the Why Can't You? Podcast

Isha Cogborn
Personal Brand Strategist, Author, Media Host, Speaker, Coach, and Community Builder

TeLisa Daughtry
Serial Social Entrepreneur, Impact Investor, and International Keynote Speaker

Glynis Devine
Bilingual Keynote Speaker, Emcee, Executive Facilitator, and Transformational Retreat Leader

Elizabeth Dillon
Motivational Speaker, Revolutionary Change Agent, and Navy Wife

Mona Dixon
International Motivational Speaker, Fundraiser, and Coach

Prince Harrison Ehimiyen
Chairman of Prince Harrison Ehimiyen Foundation Board of Directors

Klyn Elsbury
Motivational Speaker, Hypnotist and NLP Coach, Best-Selling Author, and Podcast Host

Damon Givehand
Yoga and Health Mindset Coach and Happiness Catalyst

Kiala Givehand, MFA, Ed.S
Happiness Catalyst and Empowerment Coach for Women

Travis Hardin
Inspirational Speaker and Mentor to Purpose-Seekers

Clinton Harris
CEO, Influencer, Speaker, and Entrepreneur

Dr. Micaela Herndon
Chief Executive Officer of MHerndon Enterprises, LLC

Alana M. Hill
Speaker, Author, and Consultant

Wendy Kaaki, PhD
Professor, Educational Consultant, and Mentor/Coach

Crystal Kadakia
Two-Time TEDx Speaker, Culture Change Expert, and Best-Selling Author

Ganes Kesari
Co-founder and Head of Analytics at Gramener, Inc.

Robert "Bob" Kienzle
Senior Consultant at Knowmium

Artesian D. Kirksey
Author, Transformational Speaker, and Mental Skills Coach

Vered Kogan
Executive Coach and Speaker

Tori Kruse
Founder and President of Highlights 'n Heels®, Empowerment Speaker, and Coach

Cheryl Kuba
Gerontologist, Author, and National Speaker

Sandra Long
TEDx Speaker and Author of *LinkedIn for Personal Branding*

Claudia S. Lovato
Speaker, Educator, and Professional Problem Solver

Rachael Mann
Author and Public Speaker

Bridgett McGowen
International Professional Speaker, Author, and Publisher

Dr. Will Moreland
America's #1 Leadership Life Trainer

Annette J. Morris, MA
Certified Life Coach/Business and Mental Health Coach, Author, Speaker, and EntreprenHER

Simone E. Morris
CEO, Award-Winning Diversity and Inclusion Leader, Consultant, and Speaker

Monica Neubauer
Podcaster, Speaker, and Realtor

Julie Niesen
Marketing Manager at Cisco Systems, Freelance Food Writer, Marketer, and Speaker

Robert Michael Onorato
Dean of Online Education

Chevara Orrin
Chief Creative Catalyst

Jessica M. Pierce
Founder and CEO at Career Connectors

Kelly Radi
Motivational Speaker, Award-Winning Author, and Real-Life Wonder Woman

Elaine Simpson
National Speaker, Consultant, Trainer, and Author

Jeannie Smith
Agent of Remarkable Change

Dr. Jim Smith, Jr. CSP
President and CEO at Jim Smith Jr. International

Tish Times
CEO and Founder at Tish Times Networking and Sales Training

André van Hall
The Curiosity Instigator

Kyira Wackett, MS, LPC
Therapist, Speaker, Coach, Artist Owner/Founder of Adversity Rising, LLC and Kinda Kreative, LLC

Camille R. Wallace
Founder and CEO of The Culture Company and The Culture Queen

Samantha R. White
Your Christian Mindset Educator

Terri Broussard Williams
Founder, MovementMakerTribe

About the Creator of *Own the Microphone*

Bridgett McGowen created and compiled *Own the Microphone* by bringing together the inspirational and powerful voices of 50 of the best professional speakers on the planet.

Bridgett is an award-winning international professional speaker; a 2019-2020 official member of Forbes Coaches Council; CEO of BMcTALKS Press, an independent publishing company; and the founder and owner of BMcTALKS Academy where she helps professional women be the most engaging, dynamic, incredible communicators ever!

Bridgett has been a professional speaker since 2001 and has spoken on programs alongside prominent figures such as former President Barack Obama, Deepak Chopra, Alex Rodriguez (A-Rod), Oprah Winfrey, Shonda Rhimes, Katie Couric, Chip Gaines, and Janelle Monae.

The prestigious University of Texas at Austin presented her with a Master Presenter Award in 2006; Canada-based One Woman has presented her with two Fearless Woman Awards; and she has facilitated hundreds of workshops, keynote and commencement addresses, conference sessions, trainings, and webinars to thousands of students and professionals who are positioned all around the globe.

Bridgett's expertise and presentations have been sought after by companies, post-secondary institutions, and organizations such as Society for Human Resource Management (SHRM), Vanguard Investments, Norton LifeLock, Symantec, Kentucky Fried Chicken, McGraw-Hill Education, LinkedIn Local, Association for Talent Development (ATD), Doña Ana Community College, National

Association of Women Sales Professionals, Independence University, Turnitin, and National Association of Black Accountants. She has been quoted by Transizion, has contributed to UpJourney, and has appeared as a guest on The Training and Learning Development Company's TLDCast as well as Phoenix Business Radio to showcase her expertise in the professional speaking industry. Her work in professional speaking and public speaking coaching has been highlighted by *VoyagePhoenix Magazine*; award-winning branding and consulting agency, Catalyst; The Startup Growth; and her alma mater, Prairie View A&M University (PVAMU), the second oldest institution of higher education in the state of Texas and a part of the Texas A&M University System.

Bridgett has also taught for PVAMU, Lone Star College System, and University of Phoenix. She has earned a bachelor's degree in communication and a master's degree; is a Forbes contributor; is a member of Alpha Kappa Alpha Sorority, Incorporated; is a publisher and is the 2018-2020 president of her local Toastmasters club.

In 2019, Bridgett authored and published two books, *REAL TALK: What Other Experts Won't Tell You About How to Make Presentations That Sizzle* as well as *Rise and Sizzle: Daily Communication and Presentation Strategies for Sales, Business, and Higher Ed Pros*, the former of which sold out within minutes of her presentation concluding at ATD's 76th annual international conference and exposition in Washington, D.C.

In January 2020, she also wrote and published *Show Up and Show Out: 52 Communication Habits to Make You Unforgettable*, which sold out at the annual Think Better Live Better event hosted in February 2020 in San Diego, California by *New York Times* best-sellers Marc and Angel Chernoff.

Bridgett's mission now is to help scores of professionals get the tools and skills they need to master their messages so they can turn their voices into powerhouses, inspire millions, and build serious skill sets and mindsets that will lead to more and more opportunities.

Bridgett lives with her family in the Phoenix, Arizona area, and she absolutely loves beautiful sunsets.

Post a Five-Star Amazon Review

We are so excited you have added this book to your reading collection. Please leave your honest feedback so others can see the value the book offers.

1. Visit www.amazon.com
2. Type in the search field the book title, *Own the Microphone,* along with the contributor's last name, "McGowen."
3. Scroll down, and click on "Write a customer review."

Let others know what you thought of the book and what you gained from it.

Your review will be tremendously helpful to others.

Thank you!

About BMcTALKS Press

BMcTALKS Press is an independent publishing company that provides a full suite of publishing services to new authors with an emphasis on professional speakers, professional coaches, entrepreneurs, and small business owners.

We design, create, and deliver high-quality trade books and ebooks that expand your brand, support your vision, and solidify you as a contender in your industry.

BMcTALKS Press knows professional speakers, professional coaches, entrepreneurs, and small business owners are passionate about what they do. We empower them to realize the expertise, savviness, acumen, and passion they bring to the world, and we assist them with identifying avenues for achieving the goal of becoming published authors.

When you get published, you position yourself to ...

- Add "published author" to your already impressive list of accomplishments
- Establish yourself as an authority on a topic
- Have a book that serves as an "elevated business card"
- Provide added value to your clients
- Support and expand your brand
- Give your followers another way to connect with you
- Share an important message with the world
- Position yourself to book (more) speaking engagements
- Leave a legacy
- Grow your business
- Be seen as an expert in your industry
- Make an impact

Visit **www.bmtpress.com** to schedule your complimentary, no-obligation call to discuss your book idea.

Do you already have a completed manuscript?
Submit it to **info@bmtpress.com,** and let us get to work for you.

www.ingramcontent.com/pod-product-compliance
Lightning Source LLC
Chambersburg PA
CBHW071323210326
41597CB00015B/1324